I Heard You Can Draw

Animals!

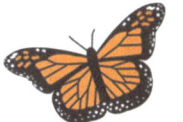

A step-by-step drawing guide

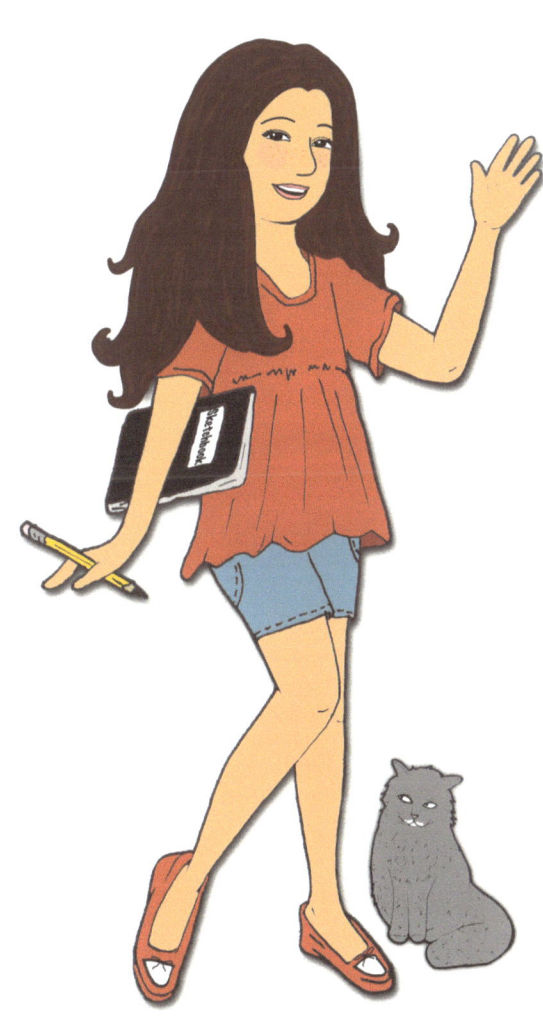

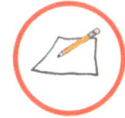

Art Class with Ms. S. Books

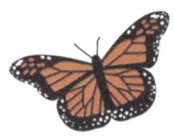

This book is for all of the kids
out there who love to draw!

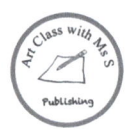

Art Class with Ms S

ISBN 13: 978-0989649025
ISBN 10: 0989649024

BISAC: Juvenile Nonfiction / Art / Drawing

I Heard You Can Draw

Animals!

A step-by-step drawing guide

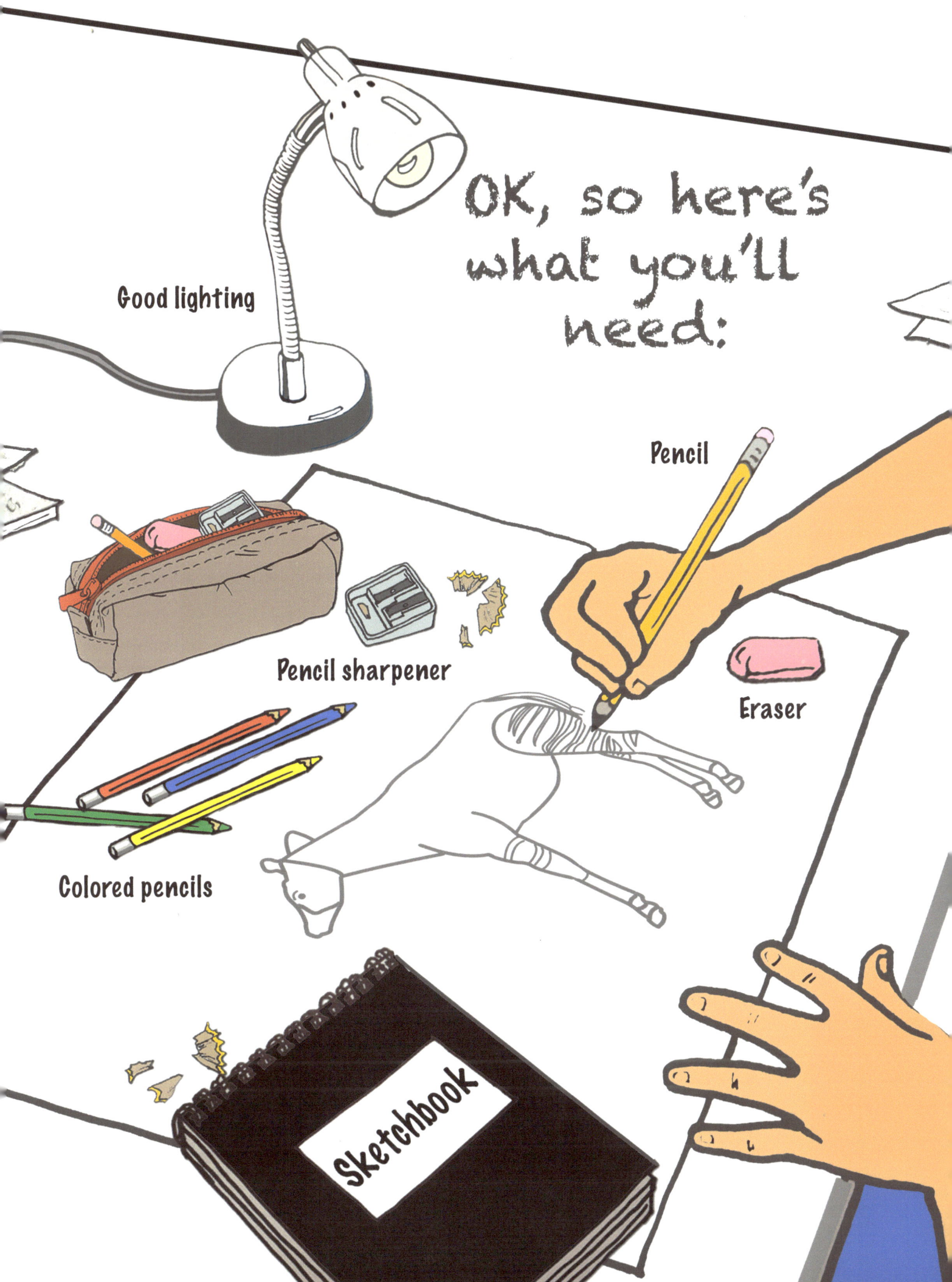

I Heard You Can Draw a...
Mallard Duck!

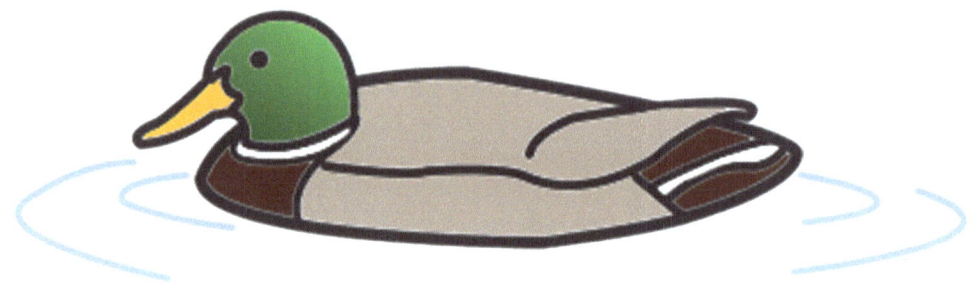

Male Mallard Ducks have a green head, a yellow bill, and a white ring around their necks. Did you know that males are called drakes and females are called hens? They migrate from the north to the south for the winter, and then back again!

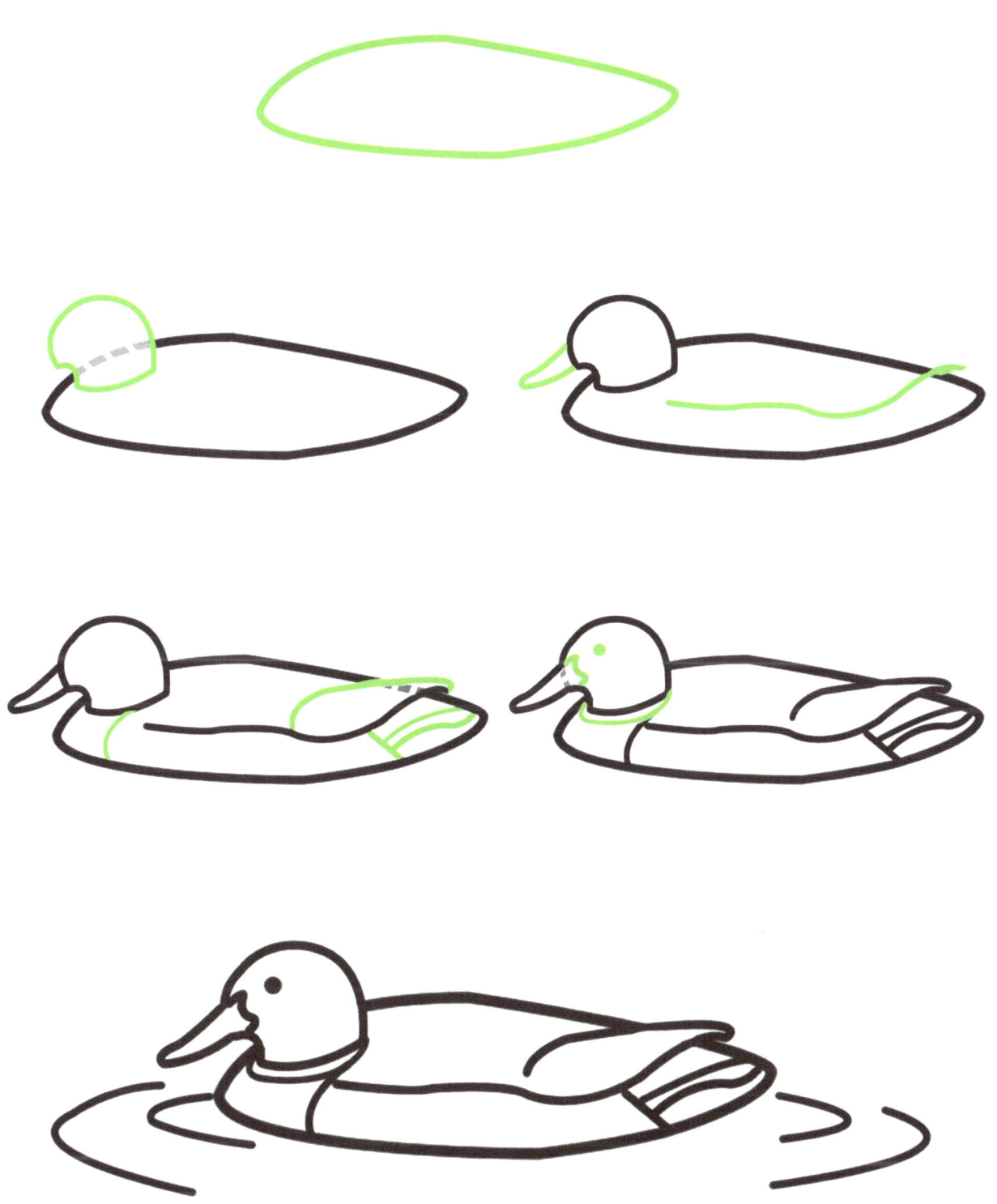

I Heard You Can Draw a...
Caribbean Flamingo!

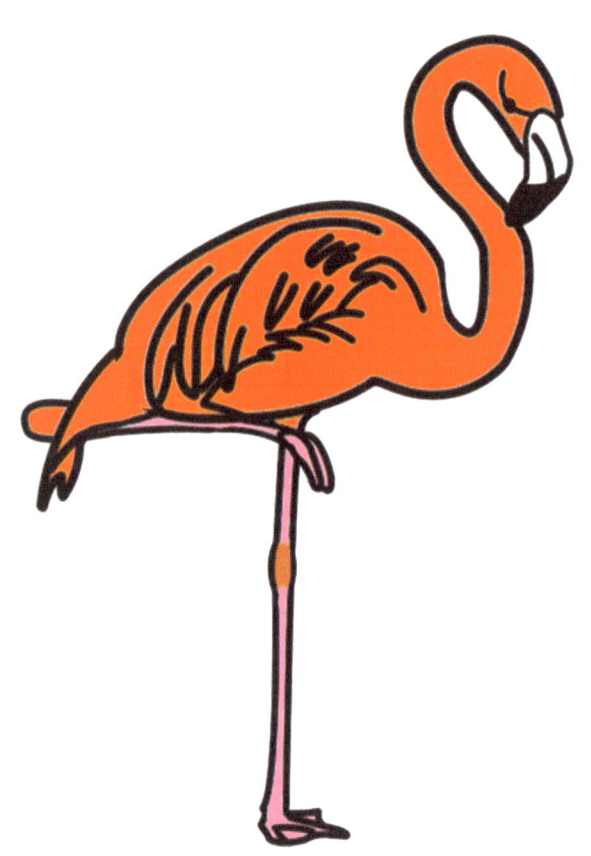

Caribbean Flamingos live in large colonies with thousands of others. They have a red/orange pink color that comes from the beta carotene in their diet of algae, small crustaceans, and insects.

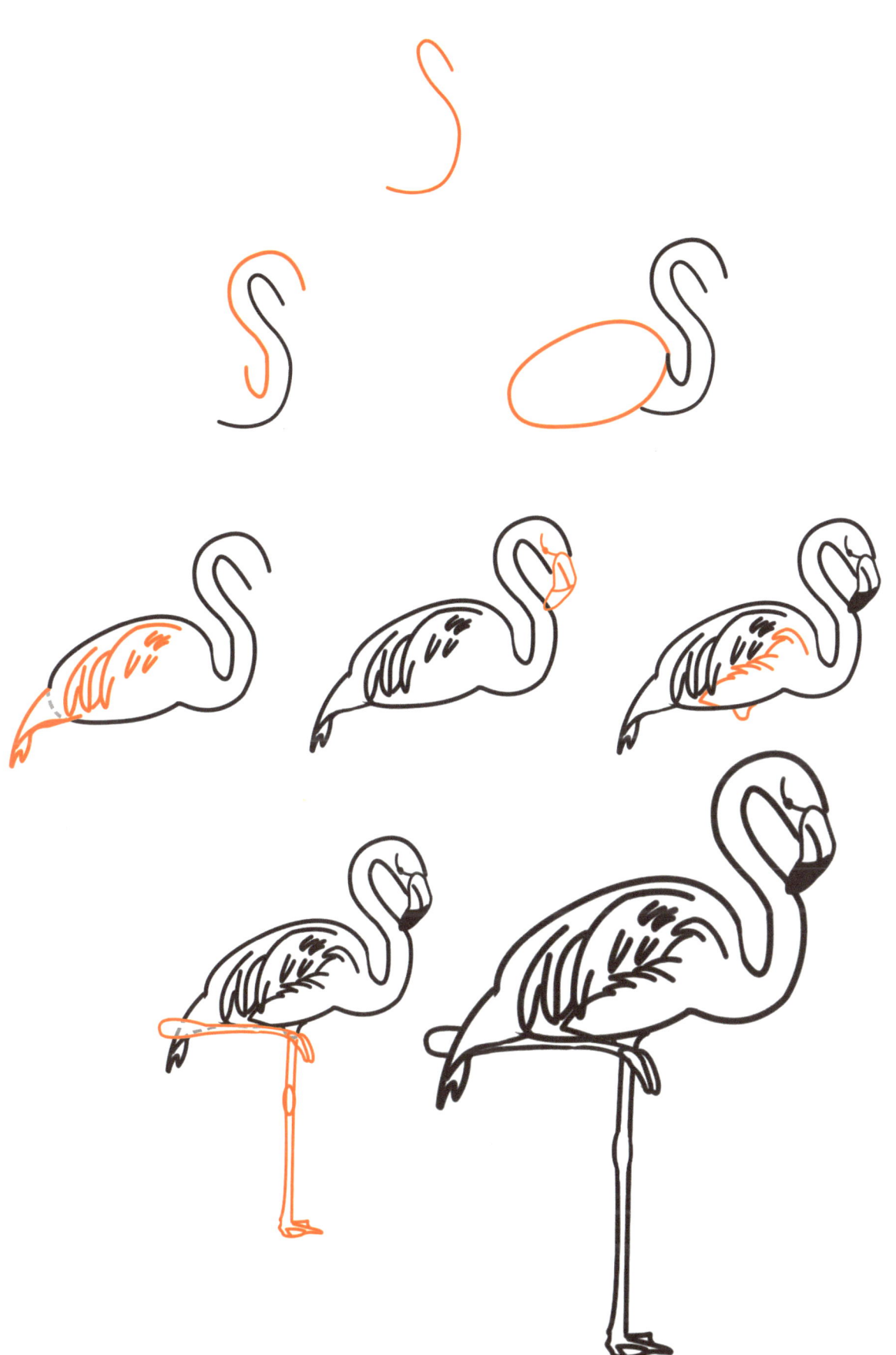

5

I Heard You Can Draw a...
Bullfrog!

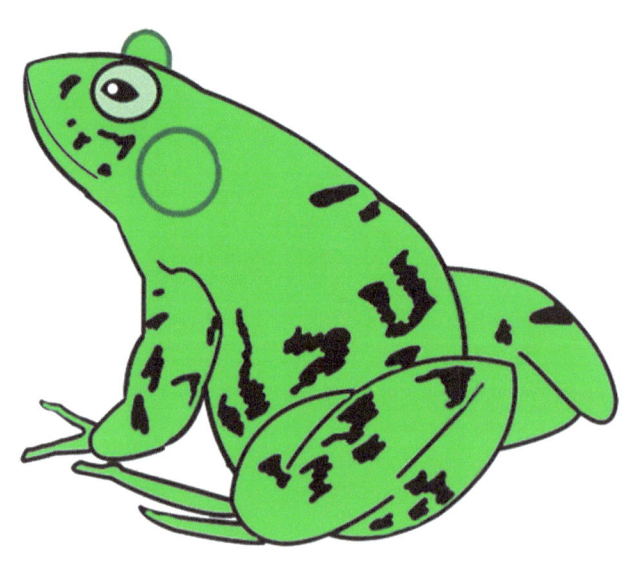

The American Bullfrog is an amphibian. An amphibian is an animal that can live on land and in water. Its life cycle starts with an egg that becomes a tadpole, which turns into a tadpole with legs, then into a frog with a tail, and then into a frog. A group of male bullfrogs is called a chorus.

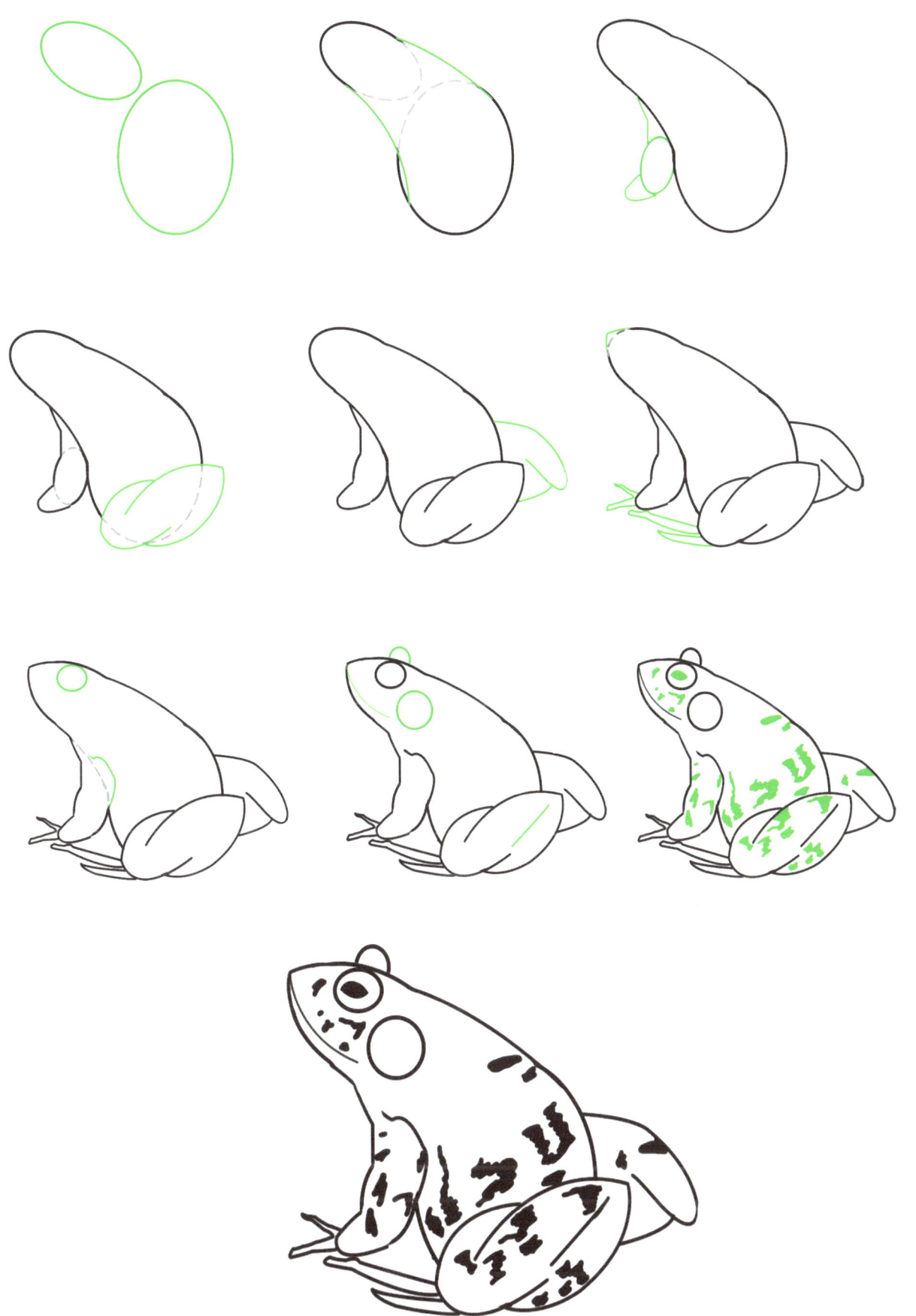

7

I Heard You Can Draw a...
Giraffe!

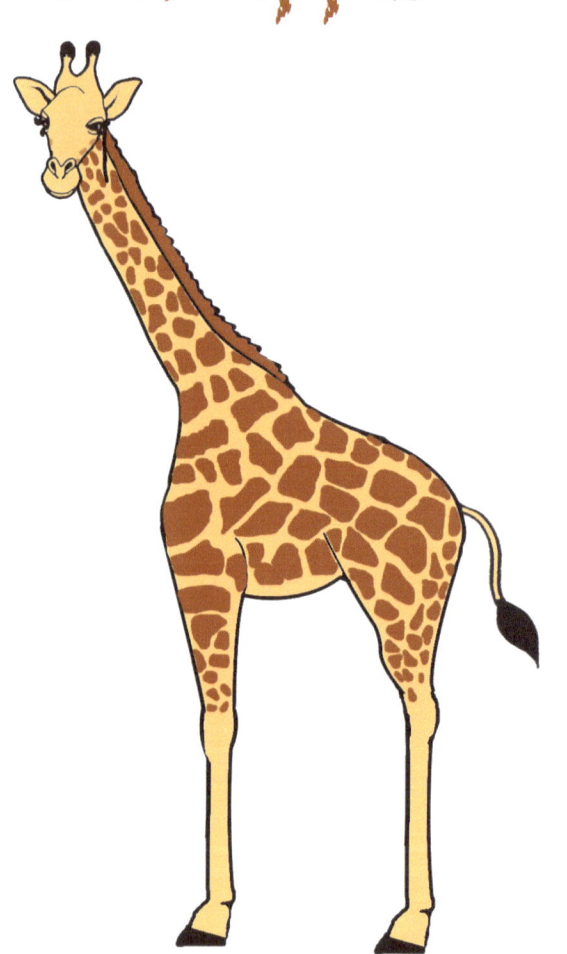

Giraffes live in African savannas. They can grow up to 18 feet tall
and a giraffe's neck and legs are both six feet tall!
Giraffes have horns on their heads called ossicones
and patches on their bodies.

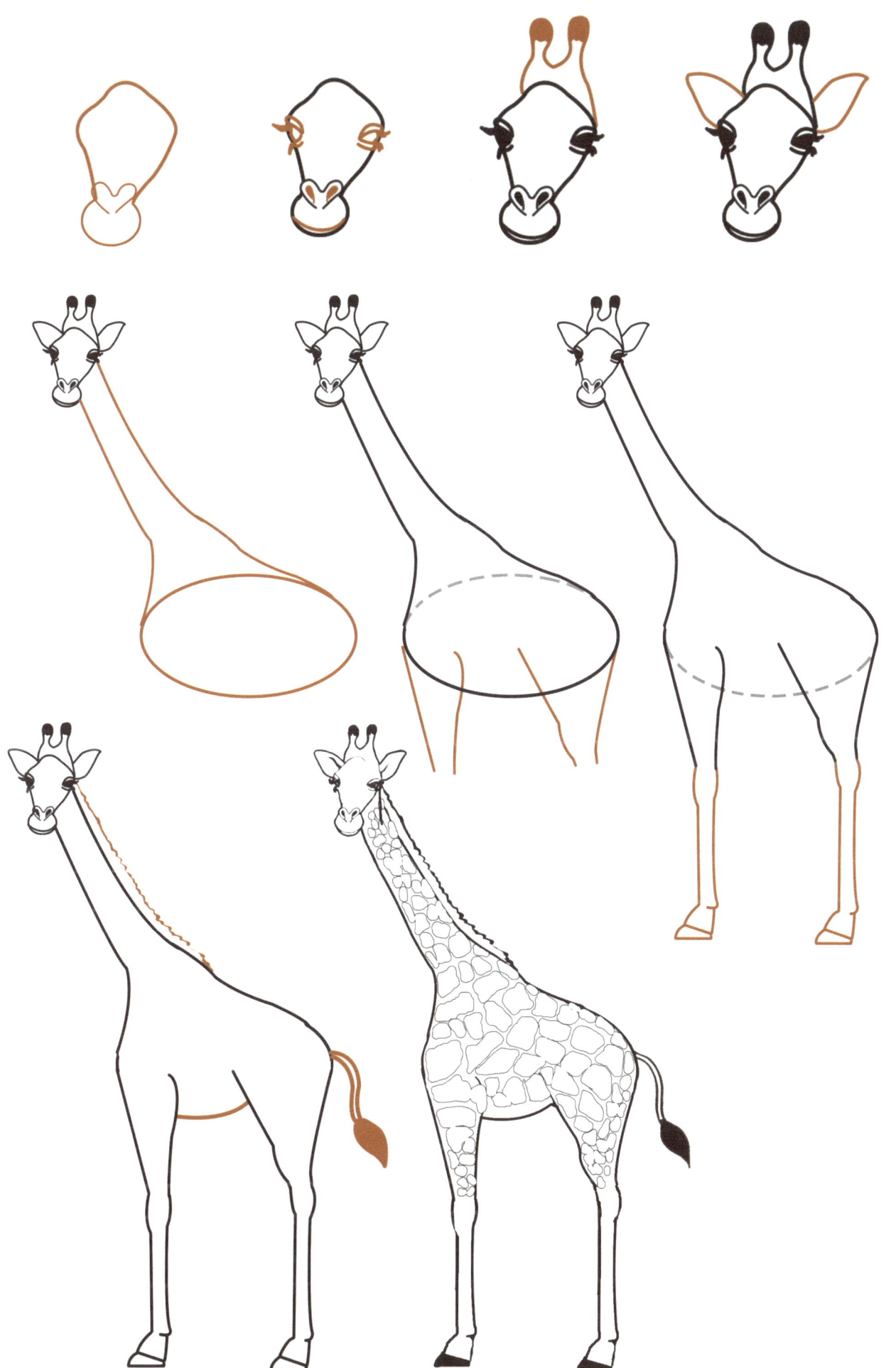

I Heard You Can Draw a...
Tabby Cat

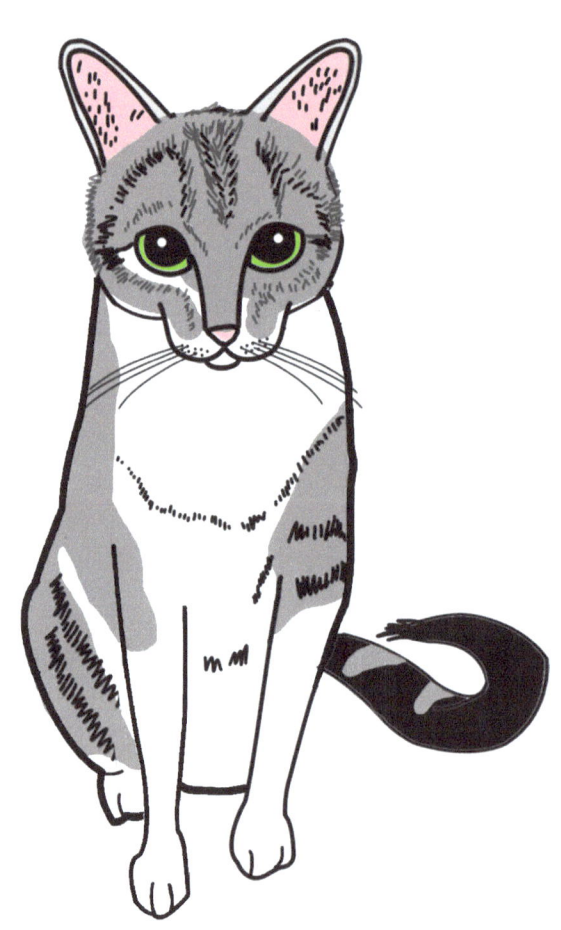

Cats are mammals. They are one of the most common house pets. Cats purr when they are happy and content!

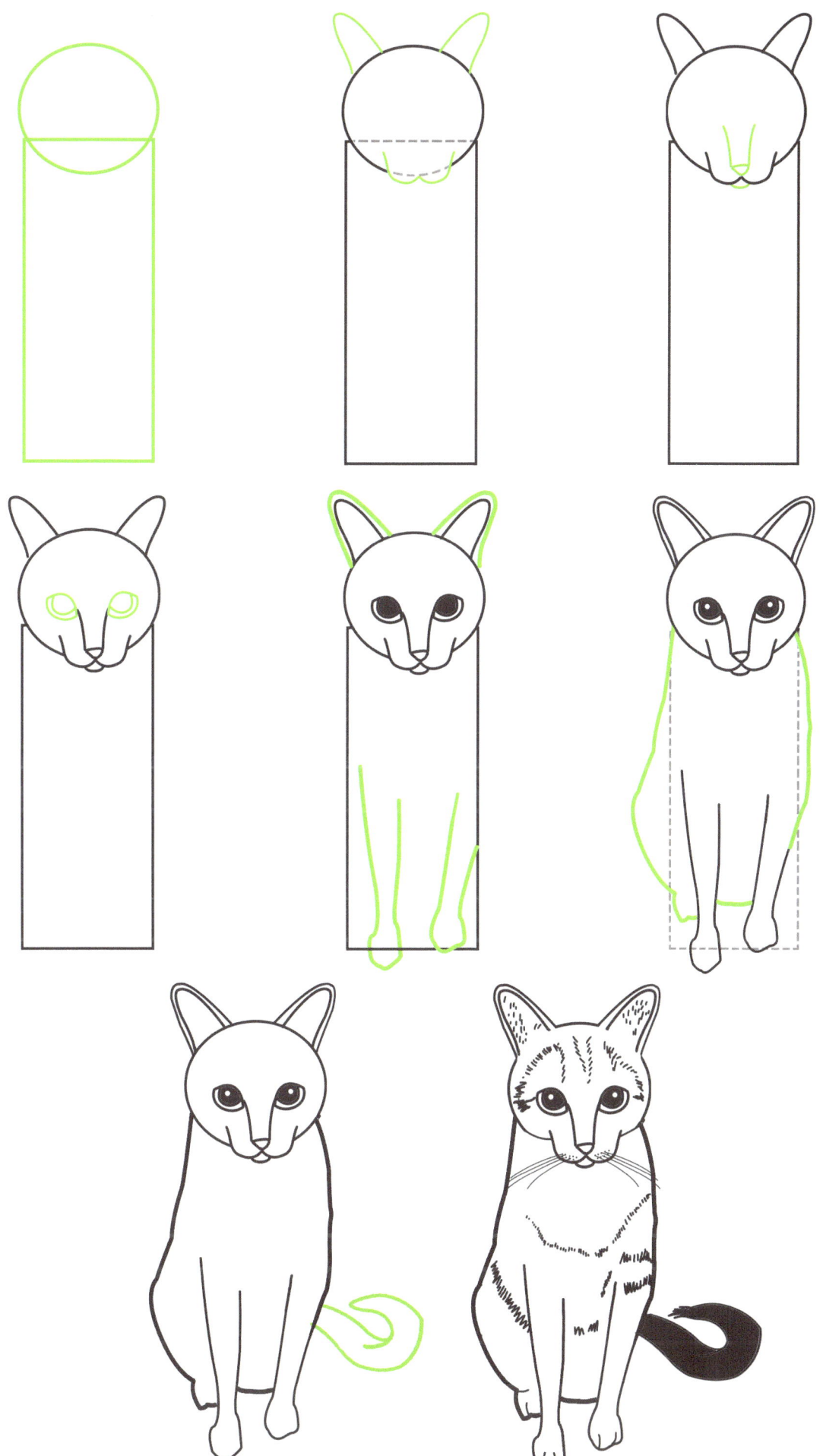

I Heard You Can Draw a...
Monarch Butterfly

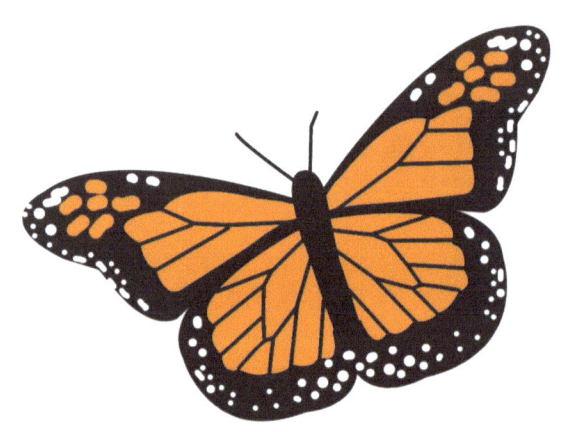

Monarch butterflies go through a life cycle in four stages:
1. Egg, 2. Larva (caterpillar), 3. Chrysalis, and 4. Butterfly.
A caterpillar hatches from an egg. Then it grows and forms a case around itself called a chrysalis. Last, it changes into a butterfly!

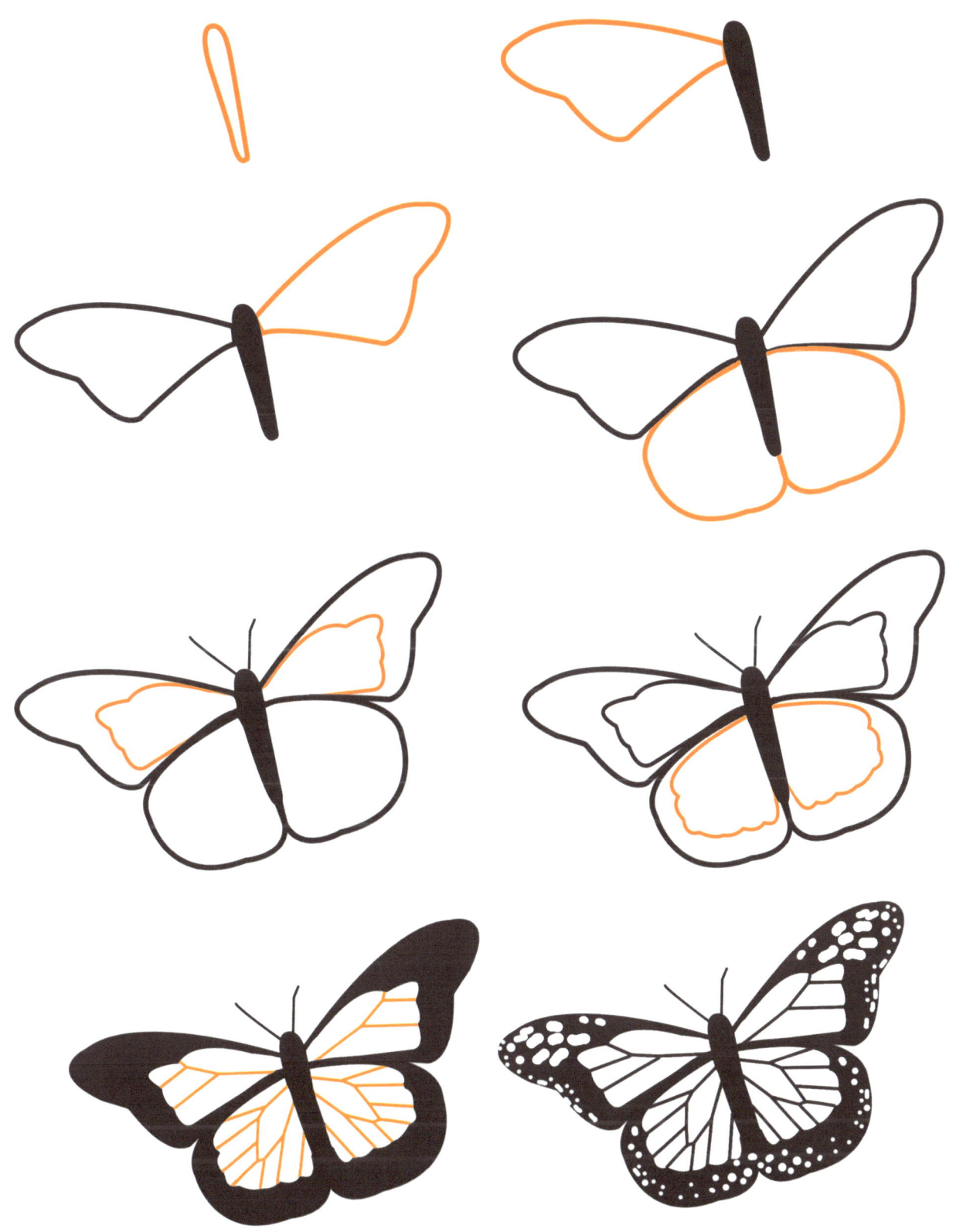

13

I Heard You Can Draw a...
Squirrel Monkey!

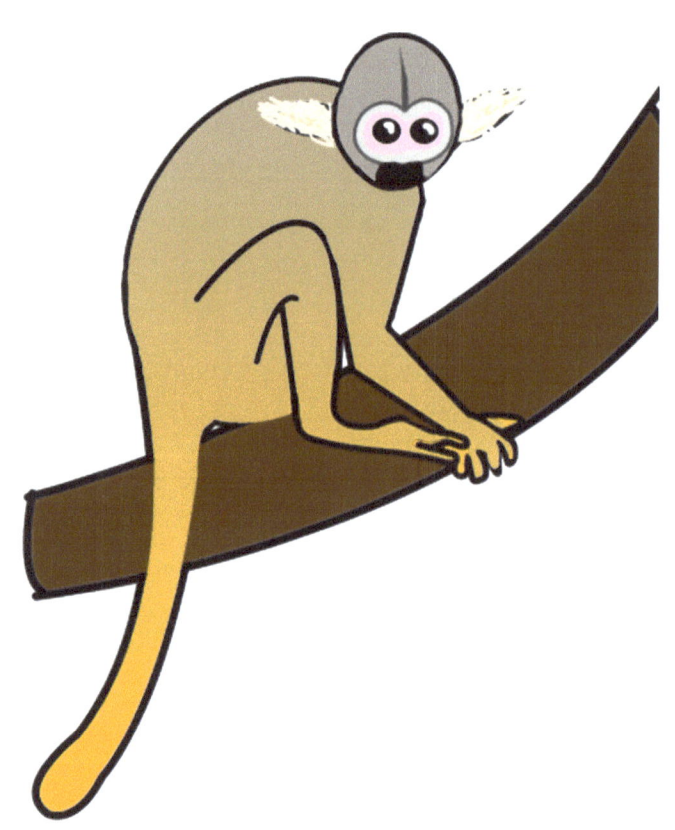

Squirrel Monkeys live in tropical rain forests in South America. They live in large groups, and eat fruit and insects.

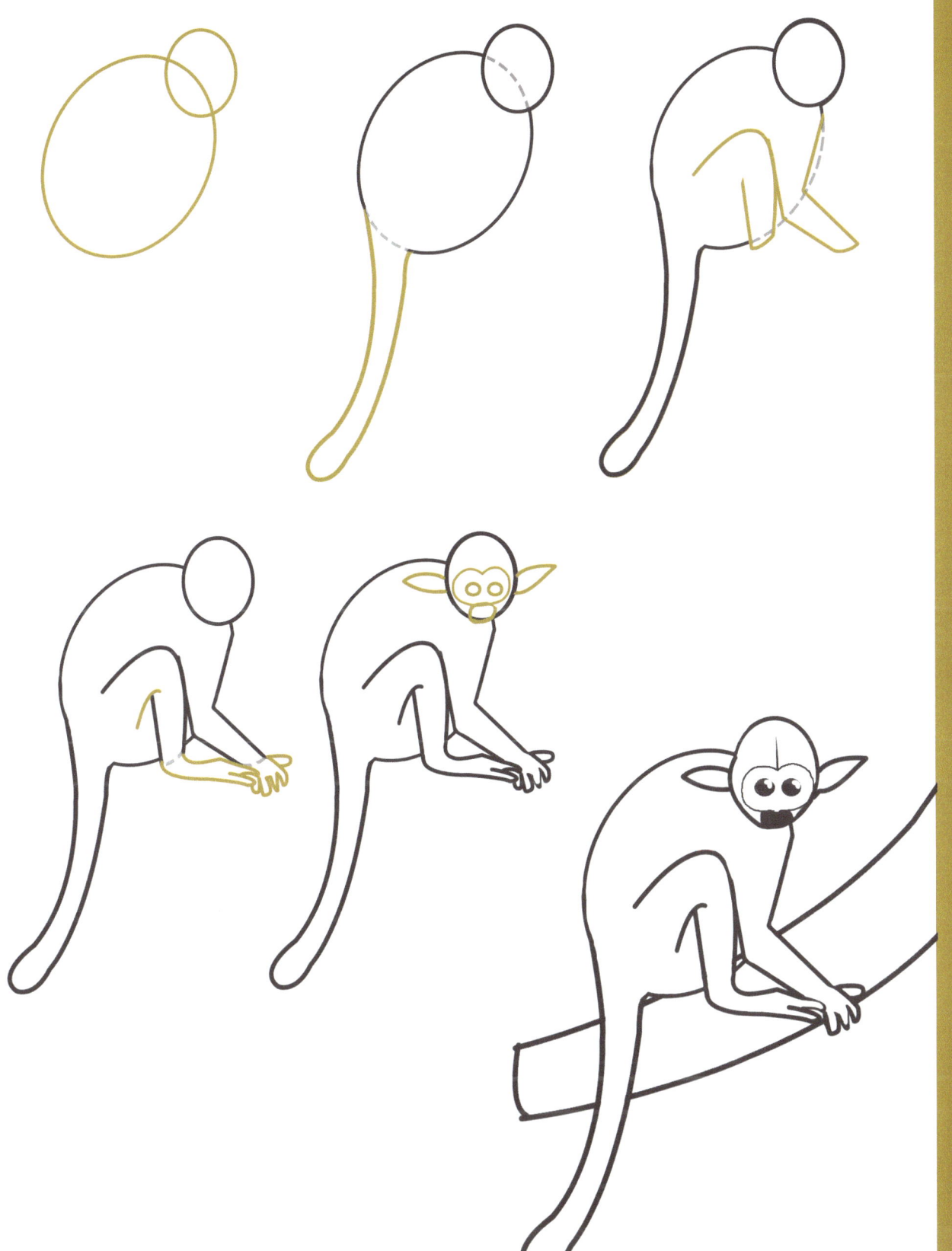

I Heard You Can Draw a...
Giant Panda!

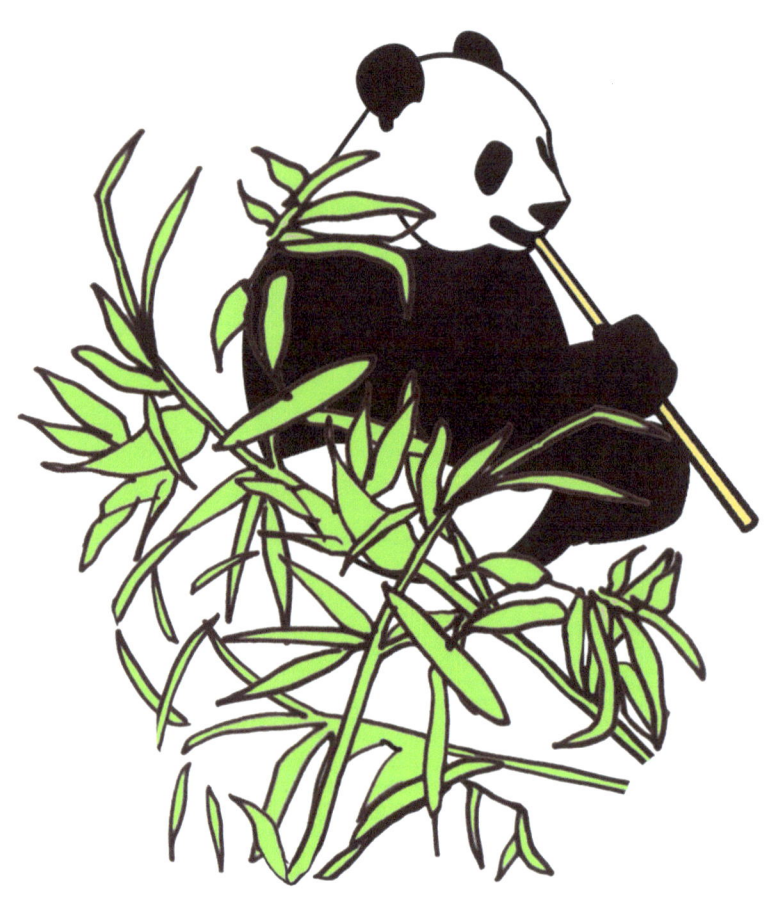

Giant Pandas are black and white bears that live in forests in China.
They mostly eat bamboo and they are considered to be endangered.

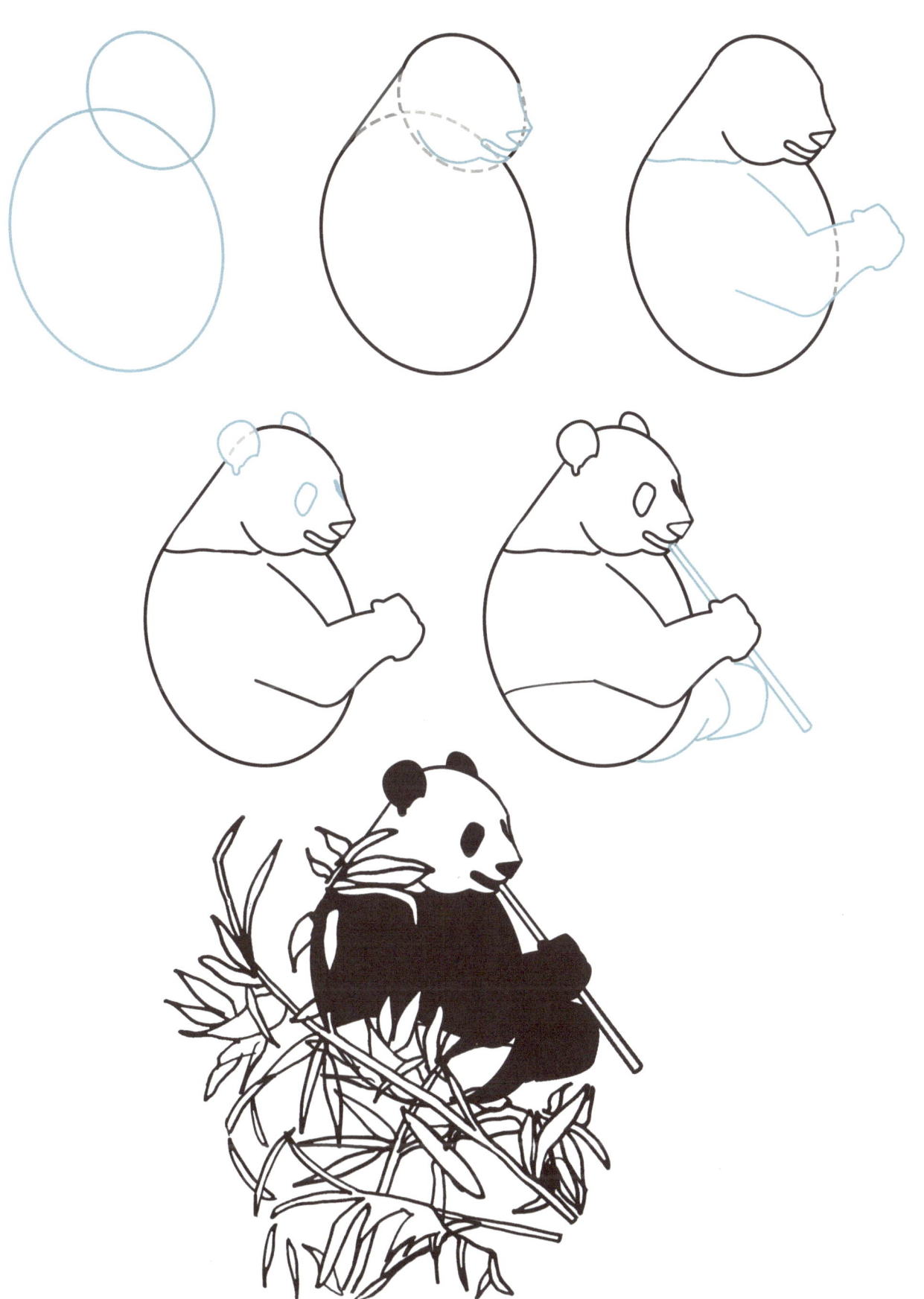

I Heard You Can Draw a...
Peacock!

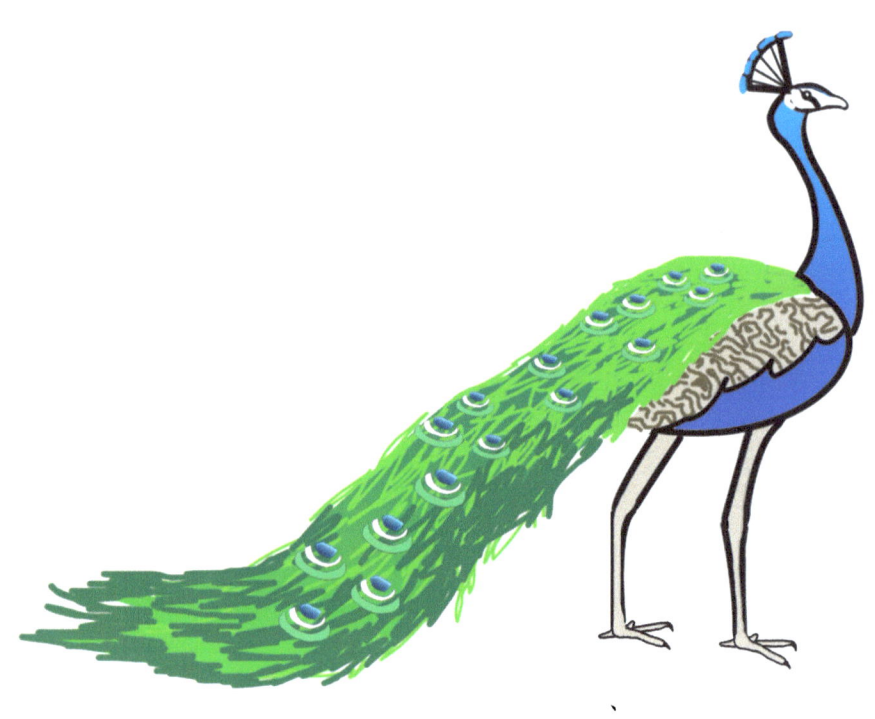

Peacocks (male) and peahens (female) are birds that are part of the pheasant family. Their babies are called peachicks. The male Indian peacock has beautiful bright blue-green feathers and a crest on the top of its head. It is the national bird of India.

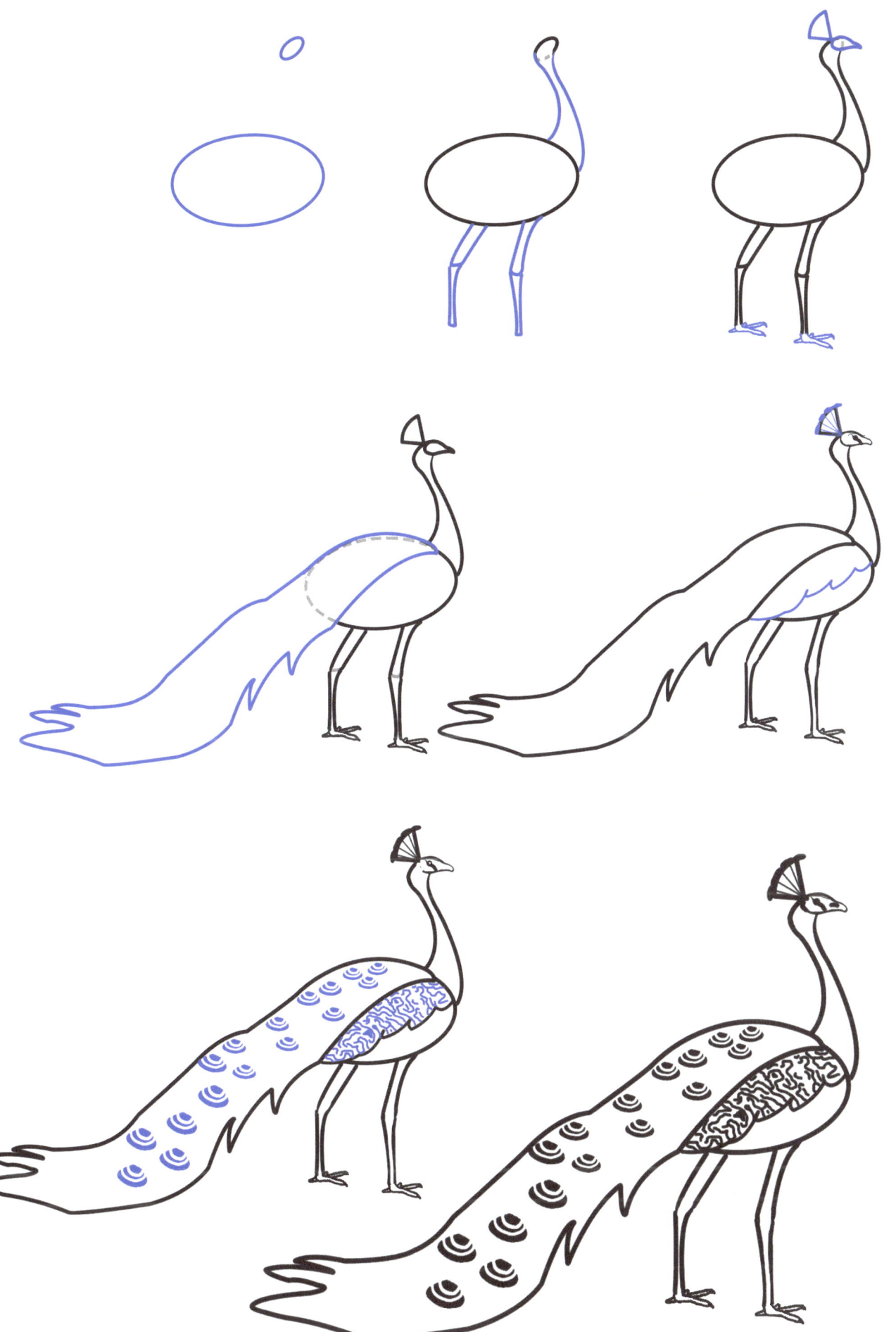

I Heard You Can Draw a...
Tortoise!

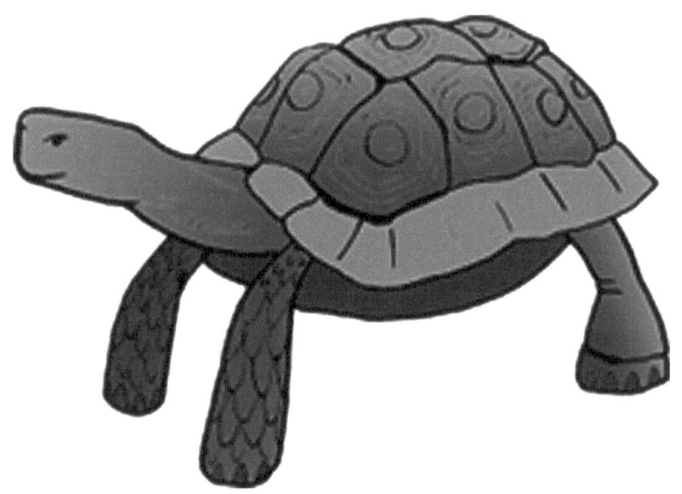

Tortoises are reptiles. Reptiles are animals that lay eggs and have cold blood. Tortoises have a shell, a long neck, and scales on their legs. They only eat plants, like grass and leaves.

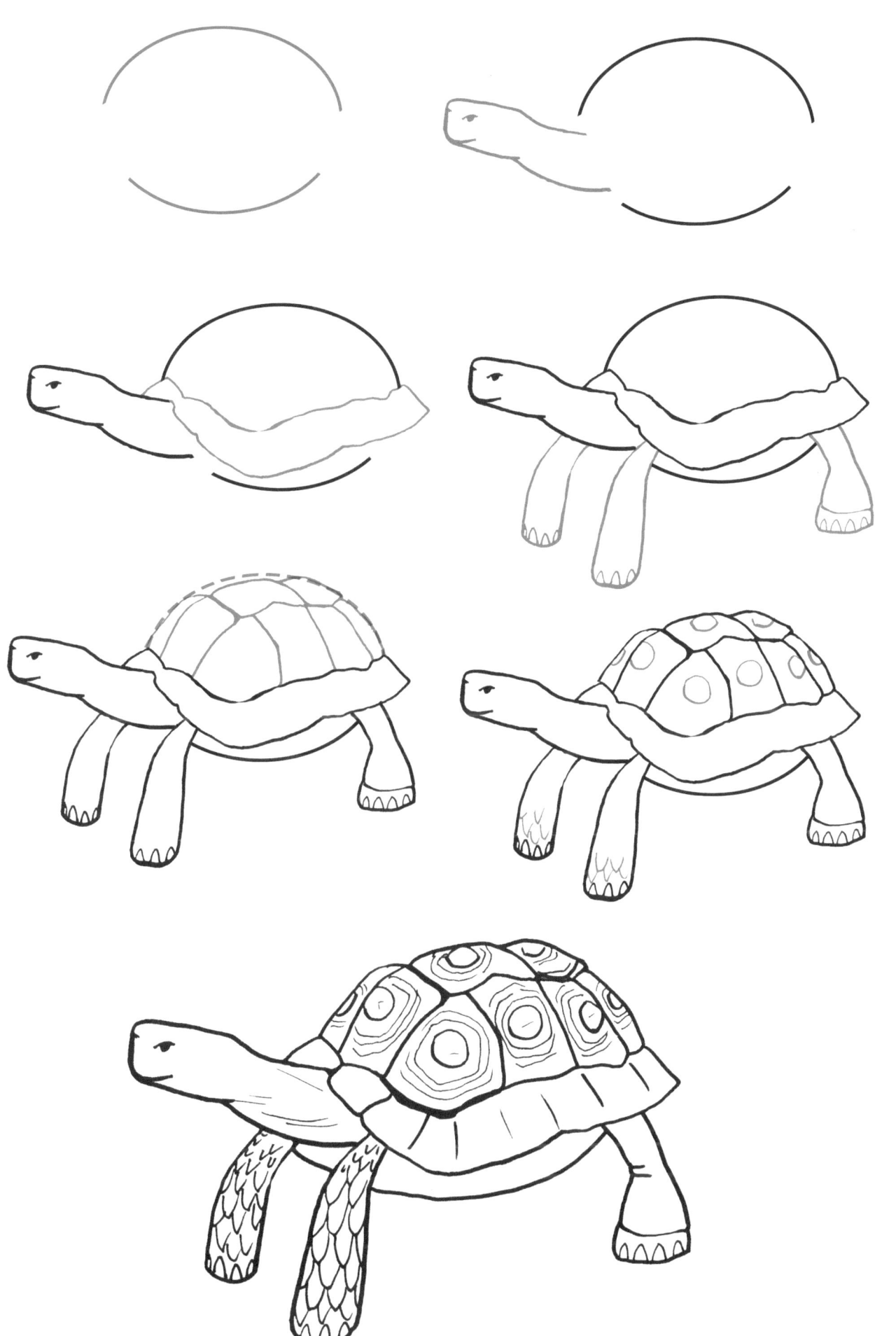

I Heard You Can Draw a...
Tiger!

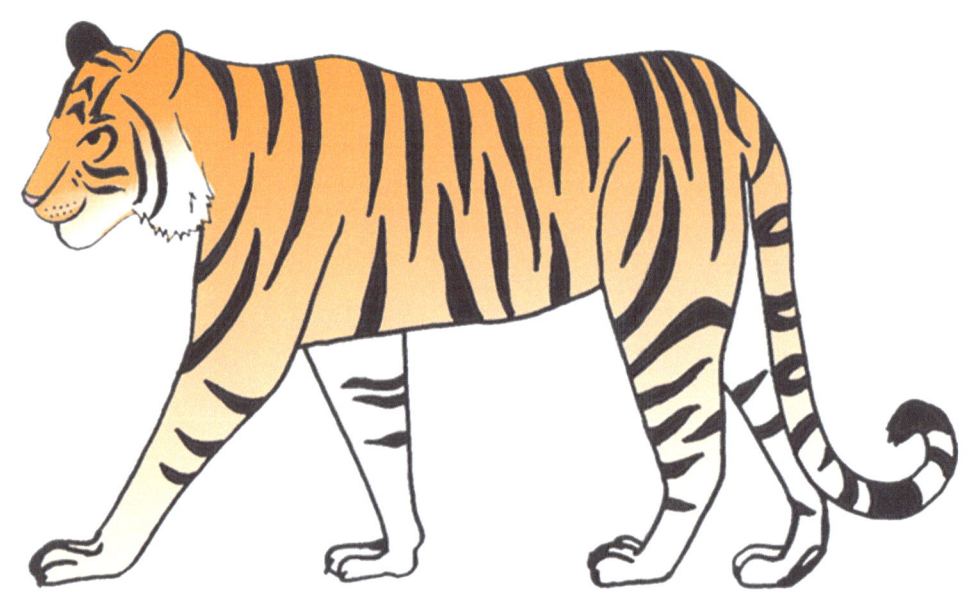

Tigers are the largest members in the cat family.
They can weigh up to 660 pounds! They hunt at night,
and they are considered to be endangered.

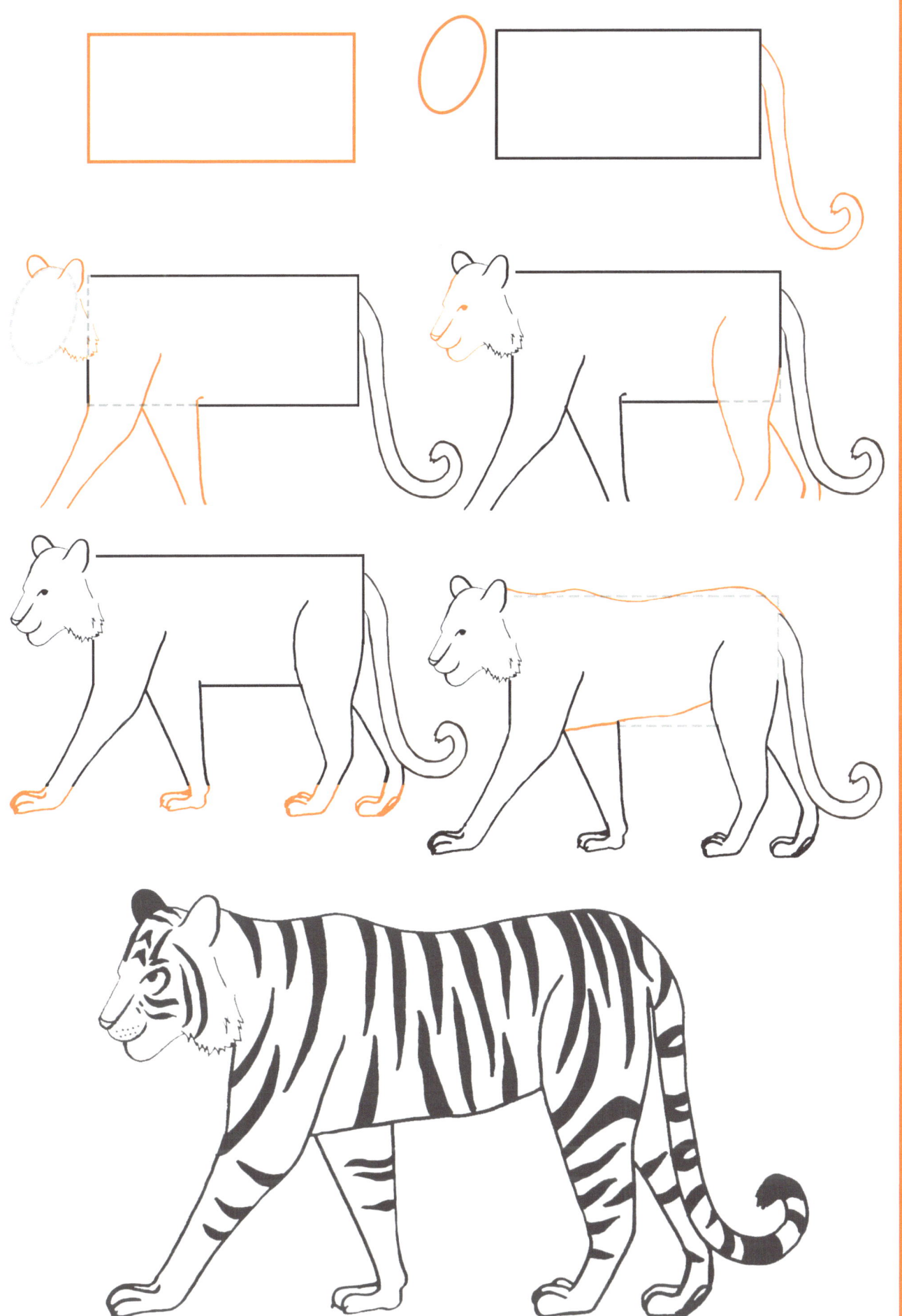

I Heard You Can Draw a...
Koala!

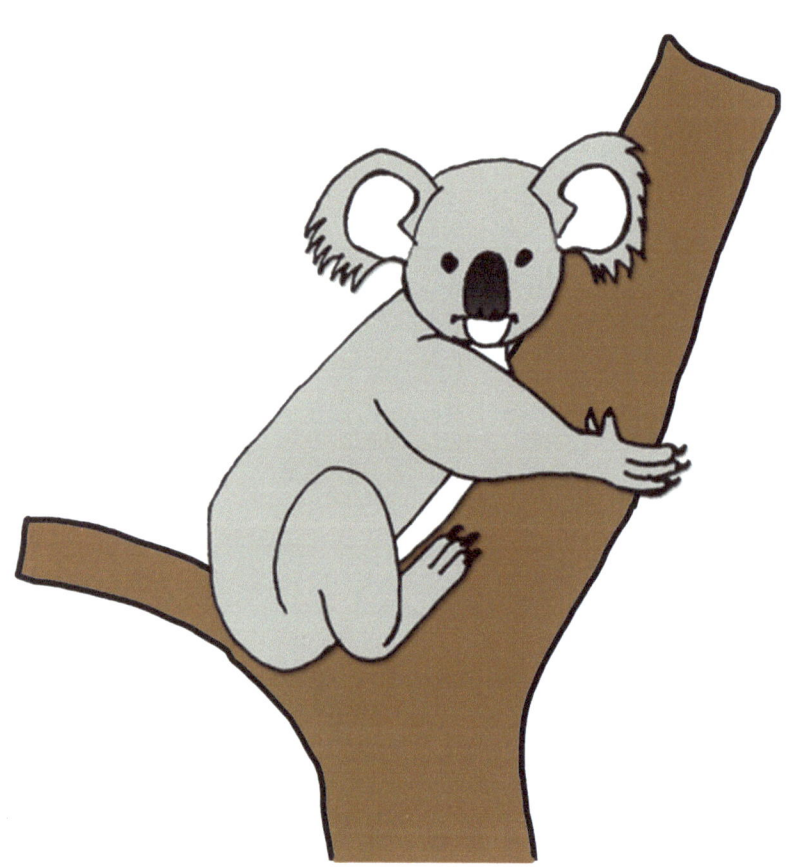

Koalas are marsupials. A marsupial is an animal that carries
its babies in a pouch on the mother's tummy. They live in Australia
and eat eucalyptus leaves from trees. They are nocturnal,
so they come out at night and sleep during the day!
Did you notice their two thumbs?

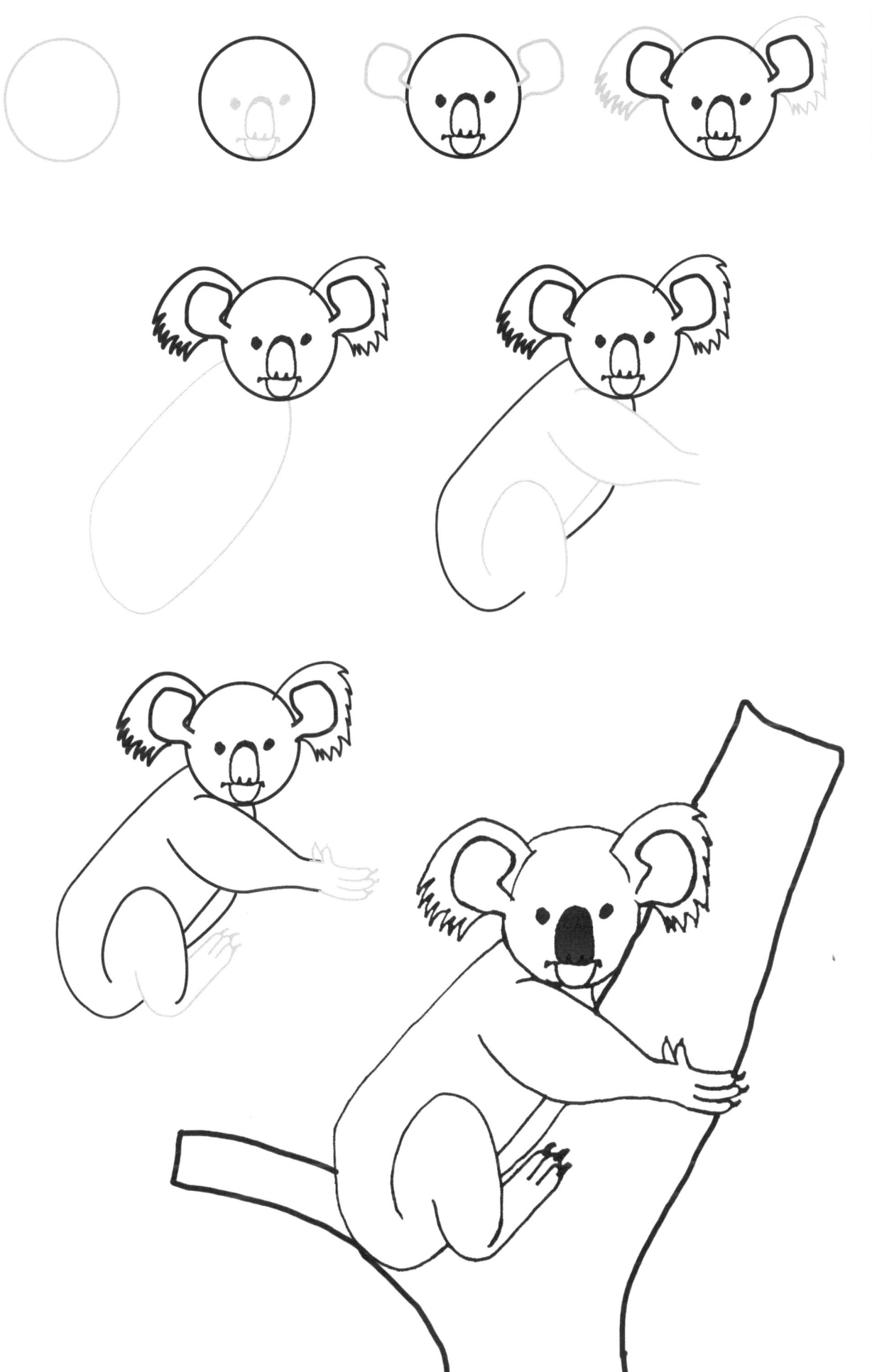

I Heard You Can Draw a...
Snail!

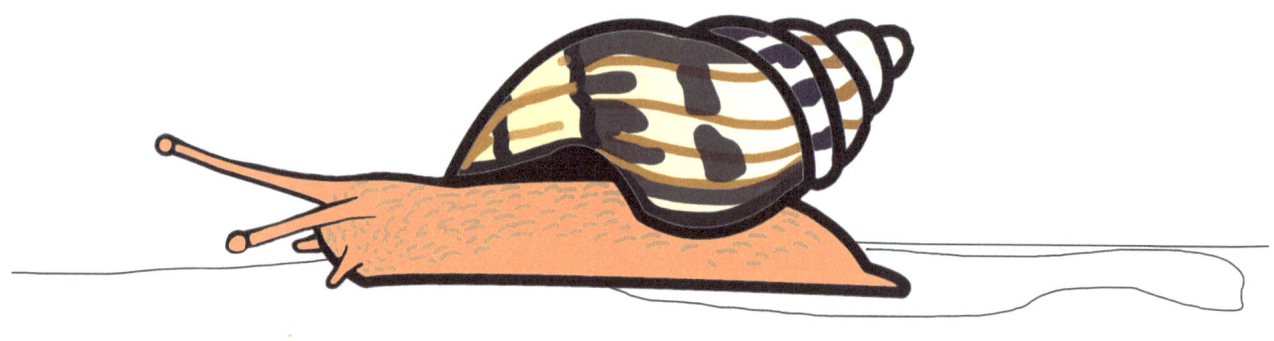

The tree snail lives in hardwood hammocks in Florida
and eats fungus and algae. As it slides along,
it leaves a layer of mucus behind!

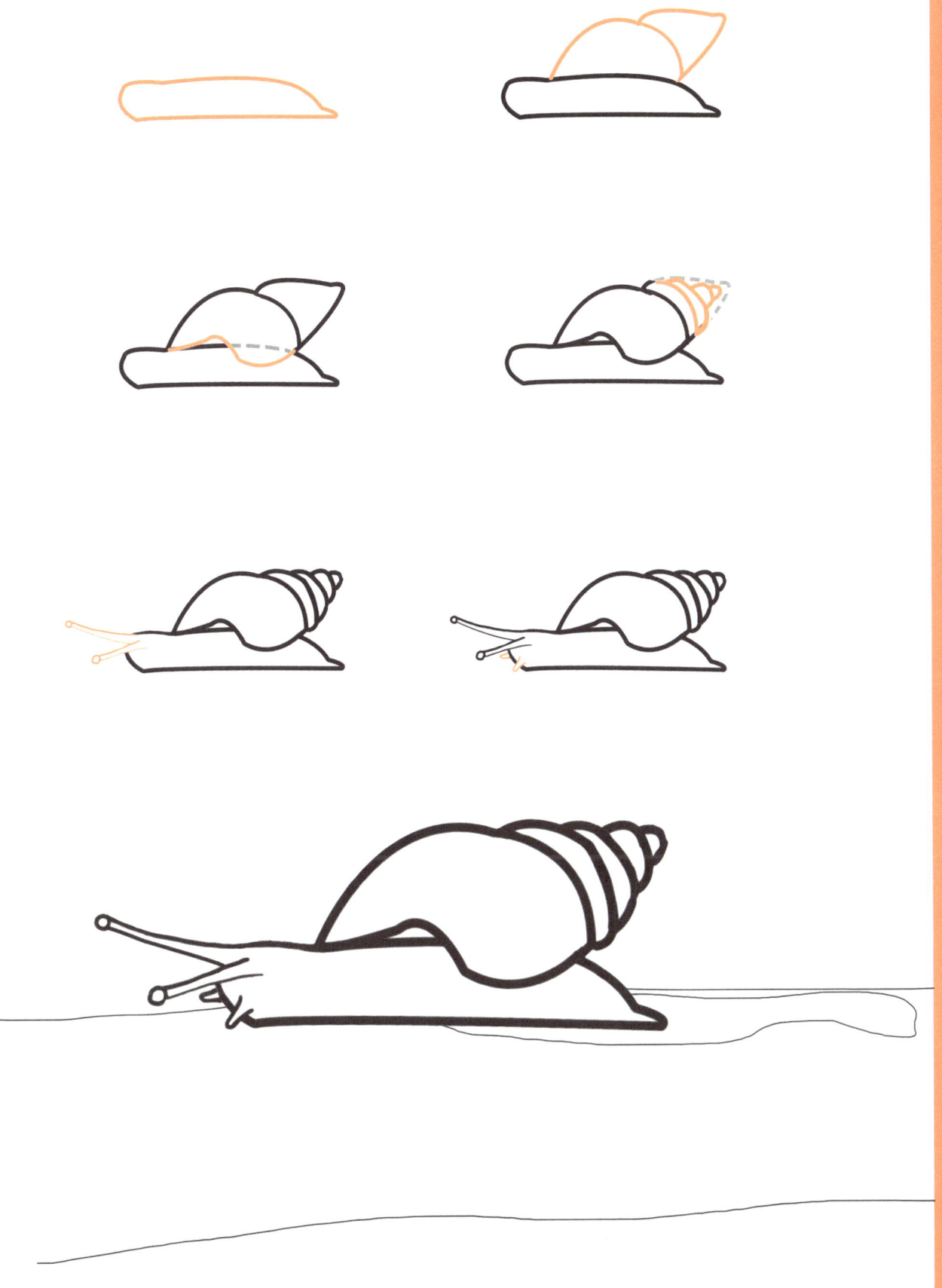

I Heard You Can Draw an...
Okapi!

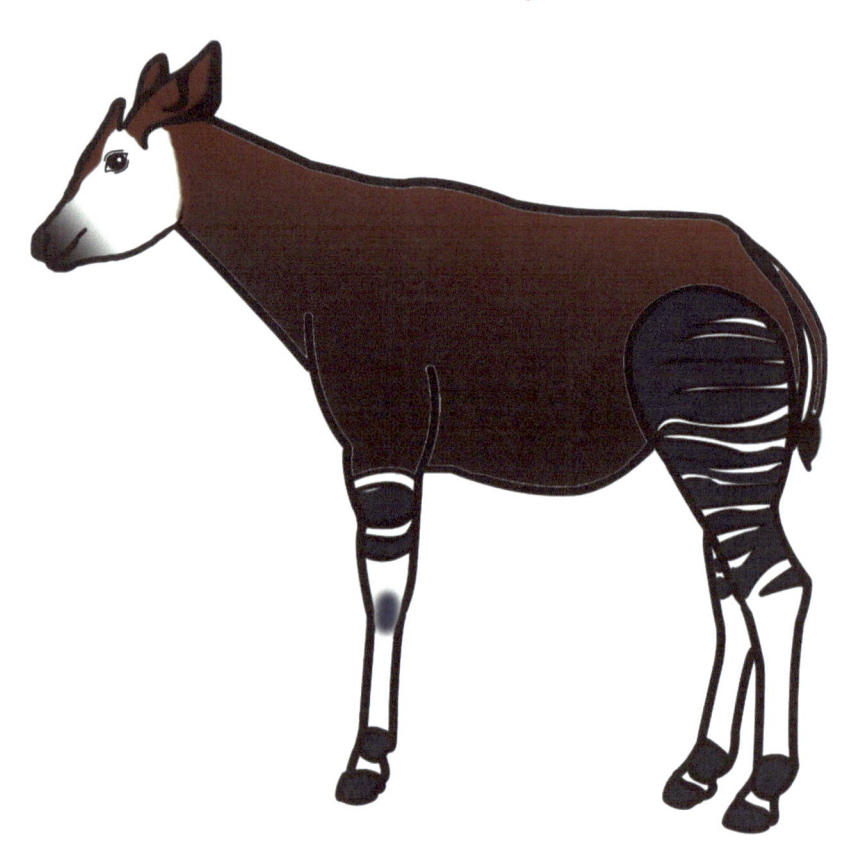

Okapis live in the Democratic Republic of Congo.
They eat fruit, leaves, and twigs. They are related to the giraffe,
although their legs look like they are part zebra!

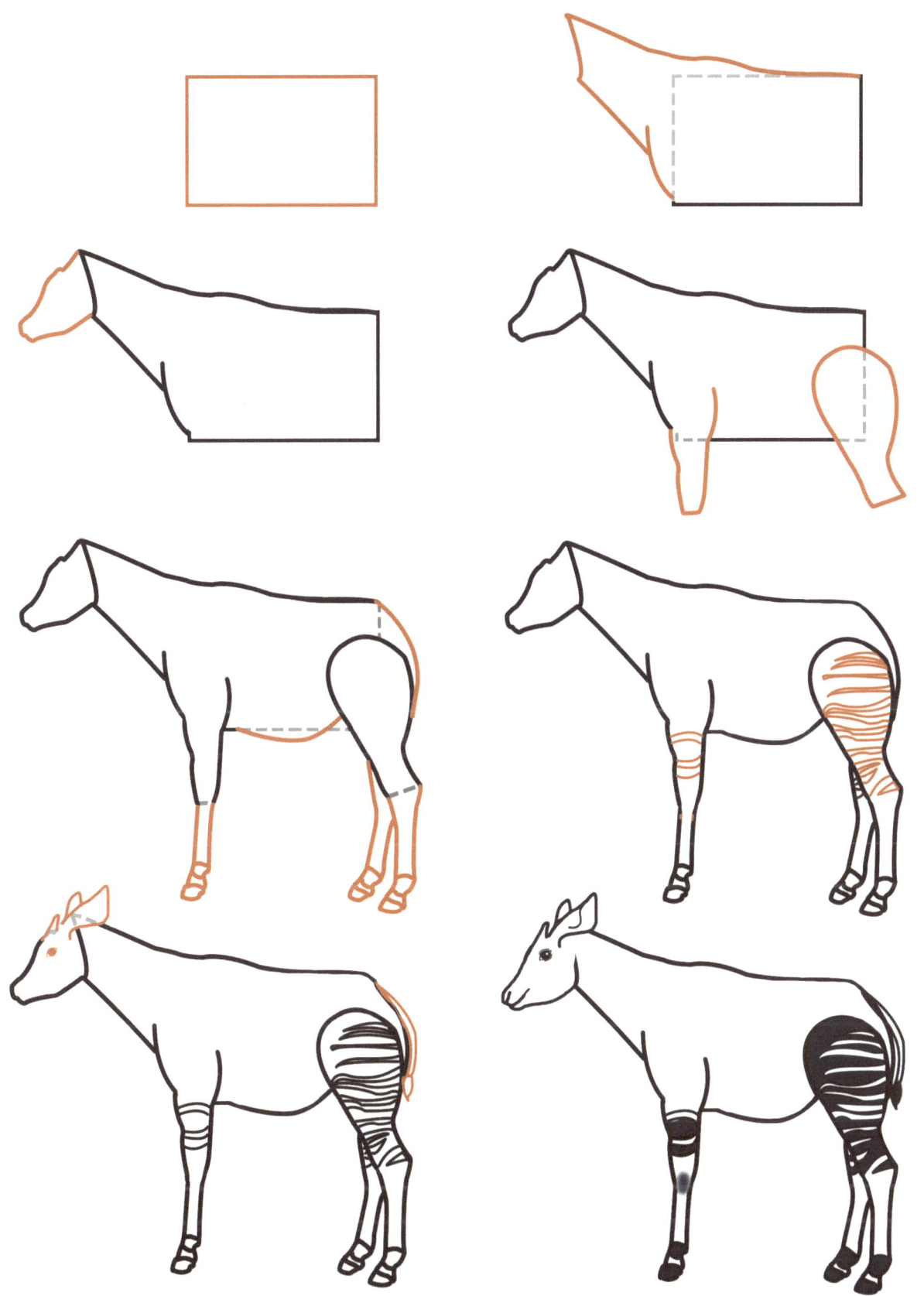

I Heard You Can Draw a...
Racket - tailed Roller!

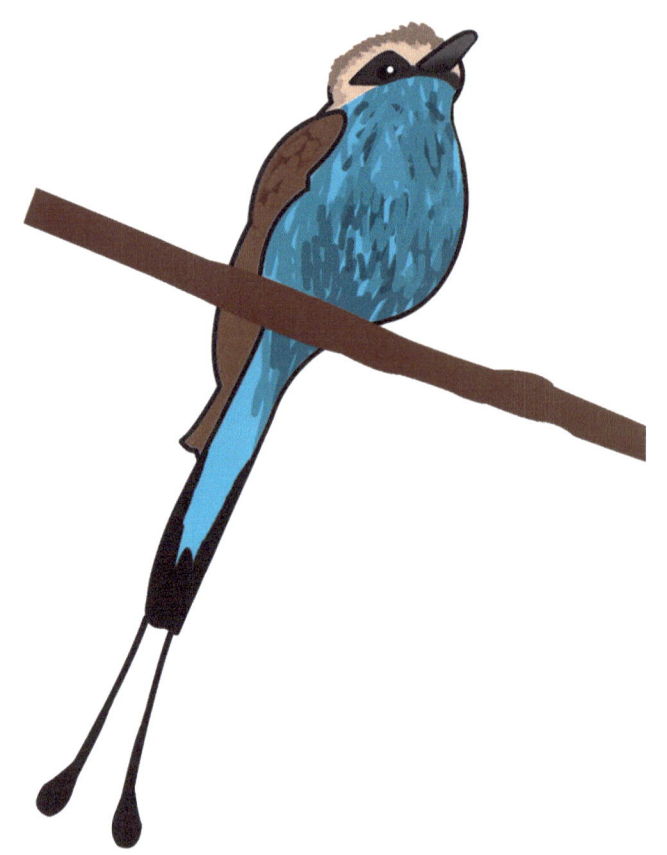

These beautiful blue bellied birds live in woodlands in
Southern Africa. They eat insects and can flip and turn in the air!

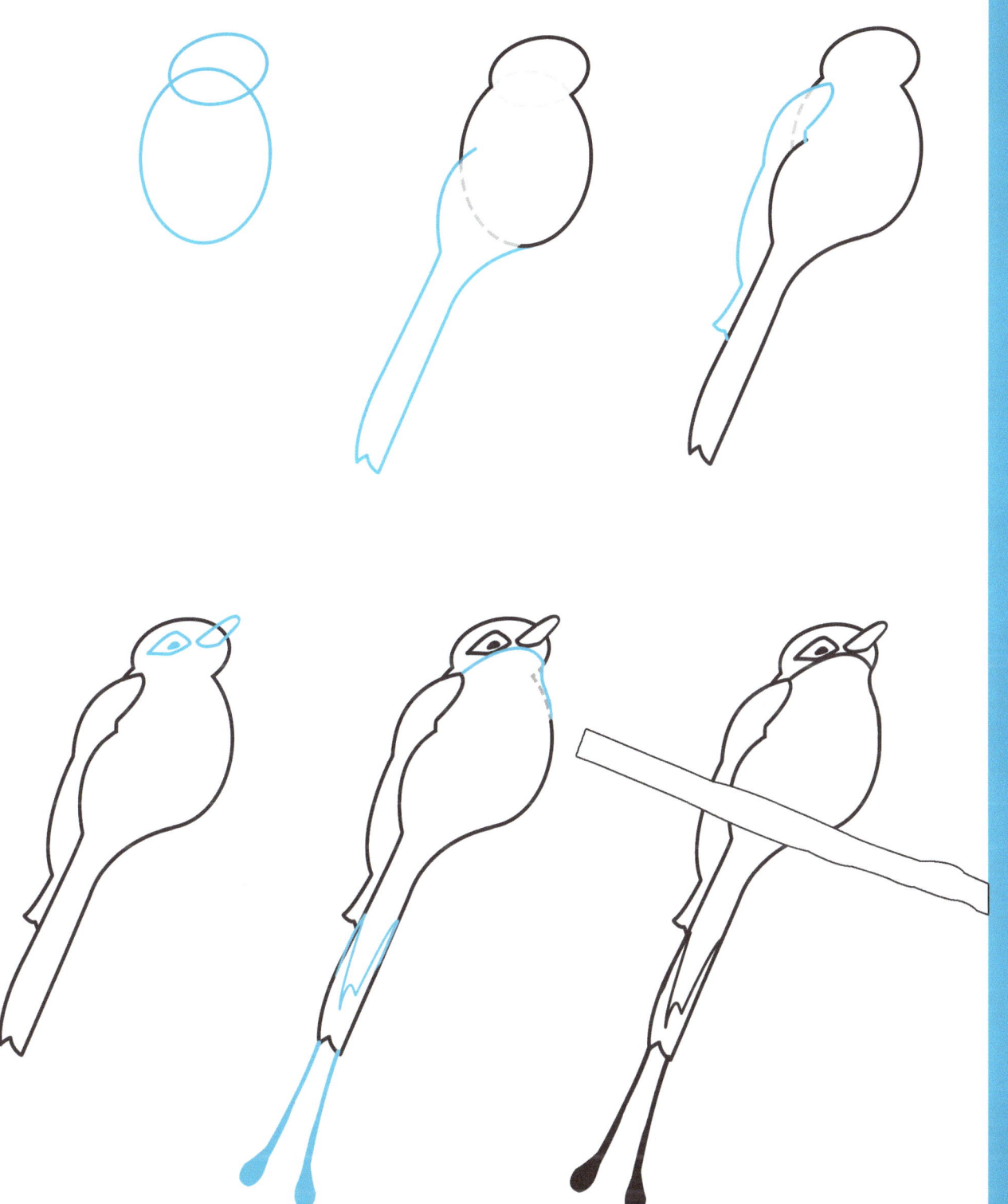

I Heard You Can Draw a...
Hummingbird!

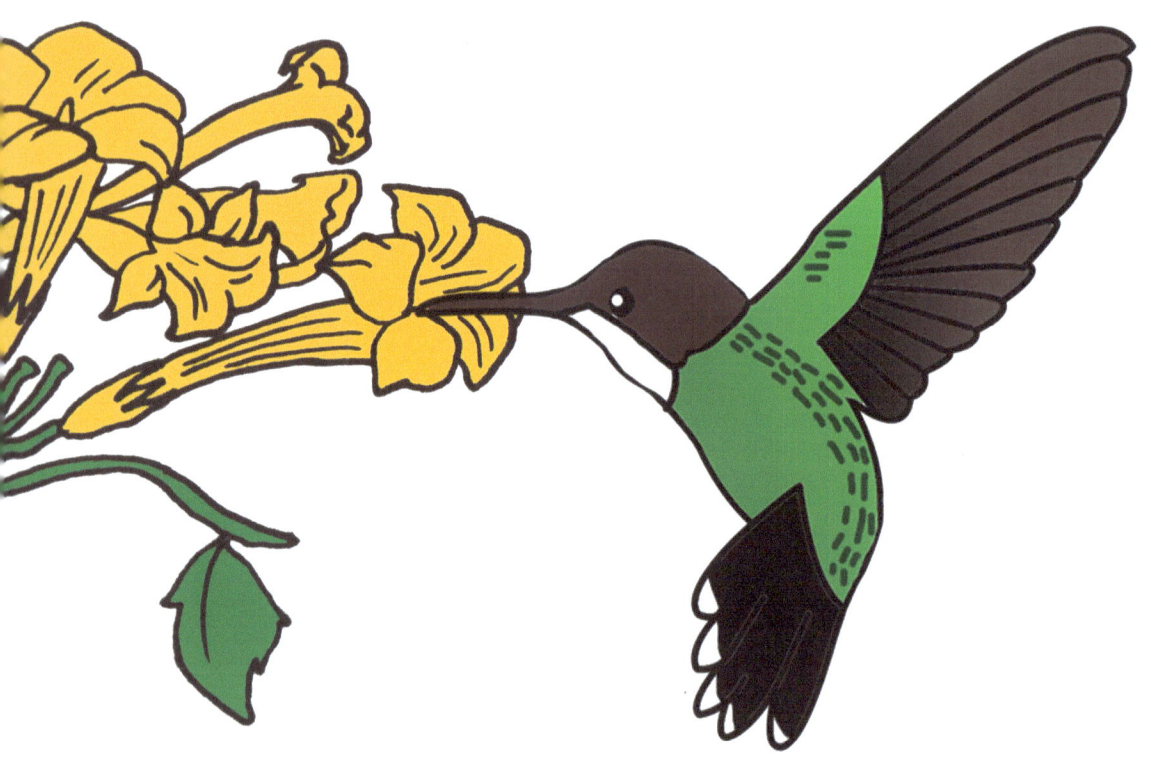

Hummingbirds are the smallest birds! Their wings make a humming noise when they are moving. They eat nectar from flowers like the Trumpet Creeper.

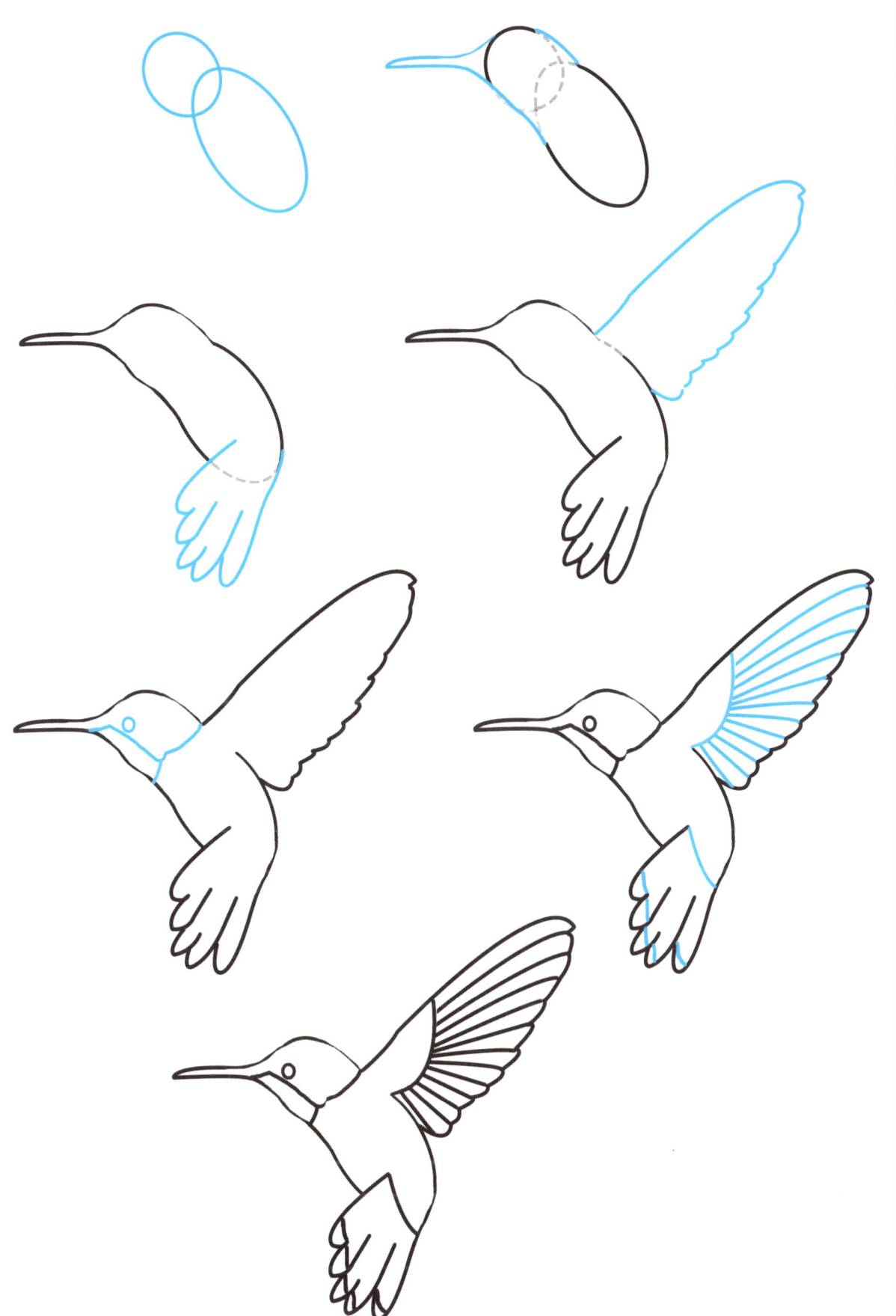

I Heard You Can Draw a...
Golden Armadillo Lizard!

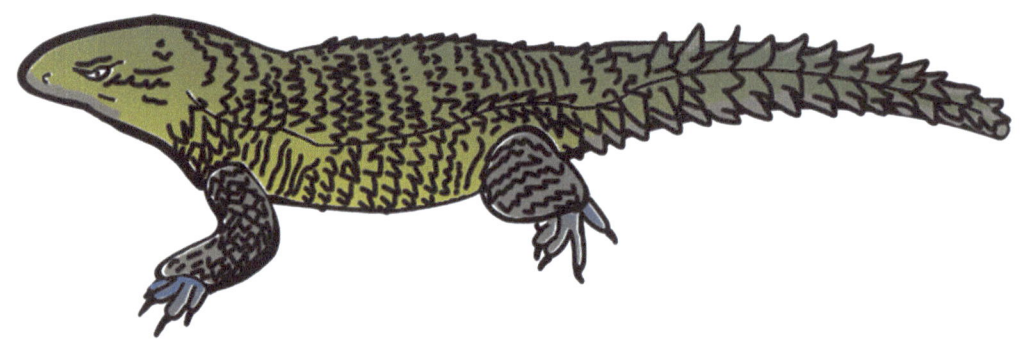

The Golden Armadillo Lizard is a reptile and lives in southern African deserts. To protect itself, it rolls into a ball with its tail in its mouth!

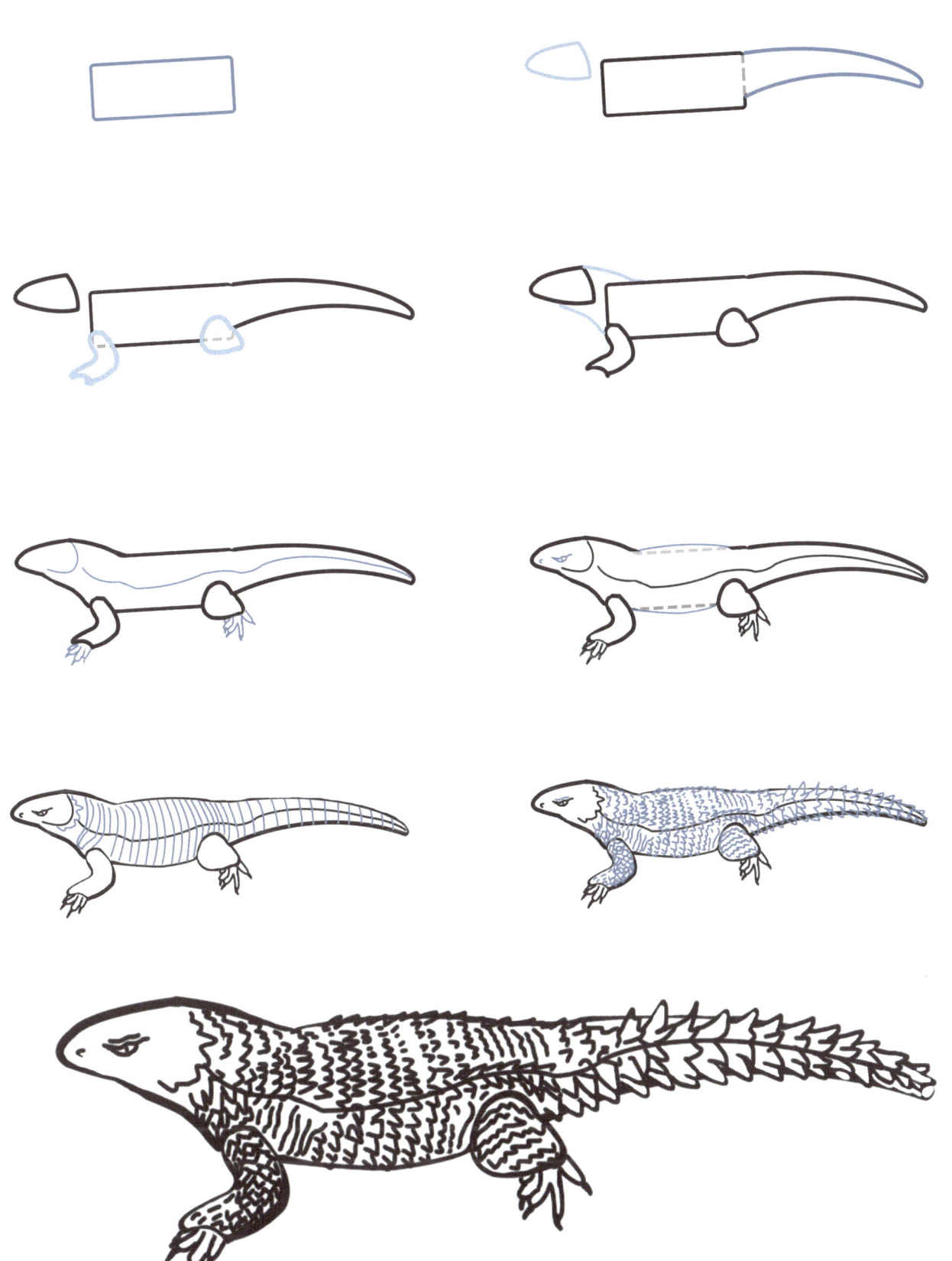

I Heard You Can Draw an...
Owl!

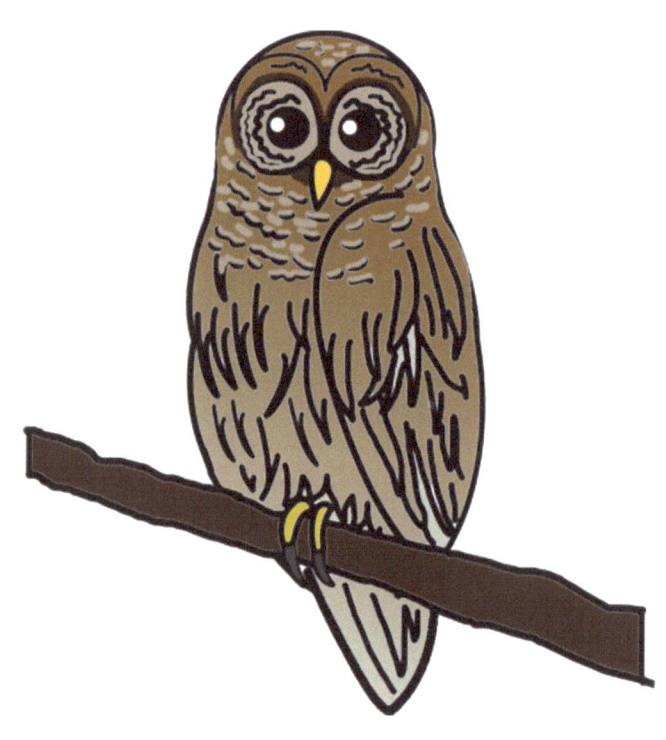

Hoo! Hoo! Barred Owls nest in holes in trees.
They live in forests and eat birds,
small mammals, reptiles and amphibians.

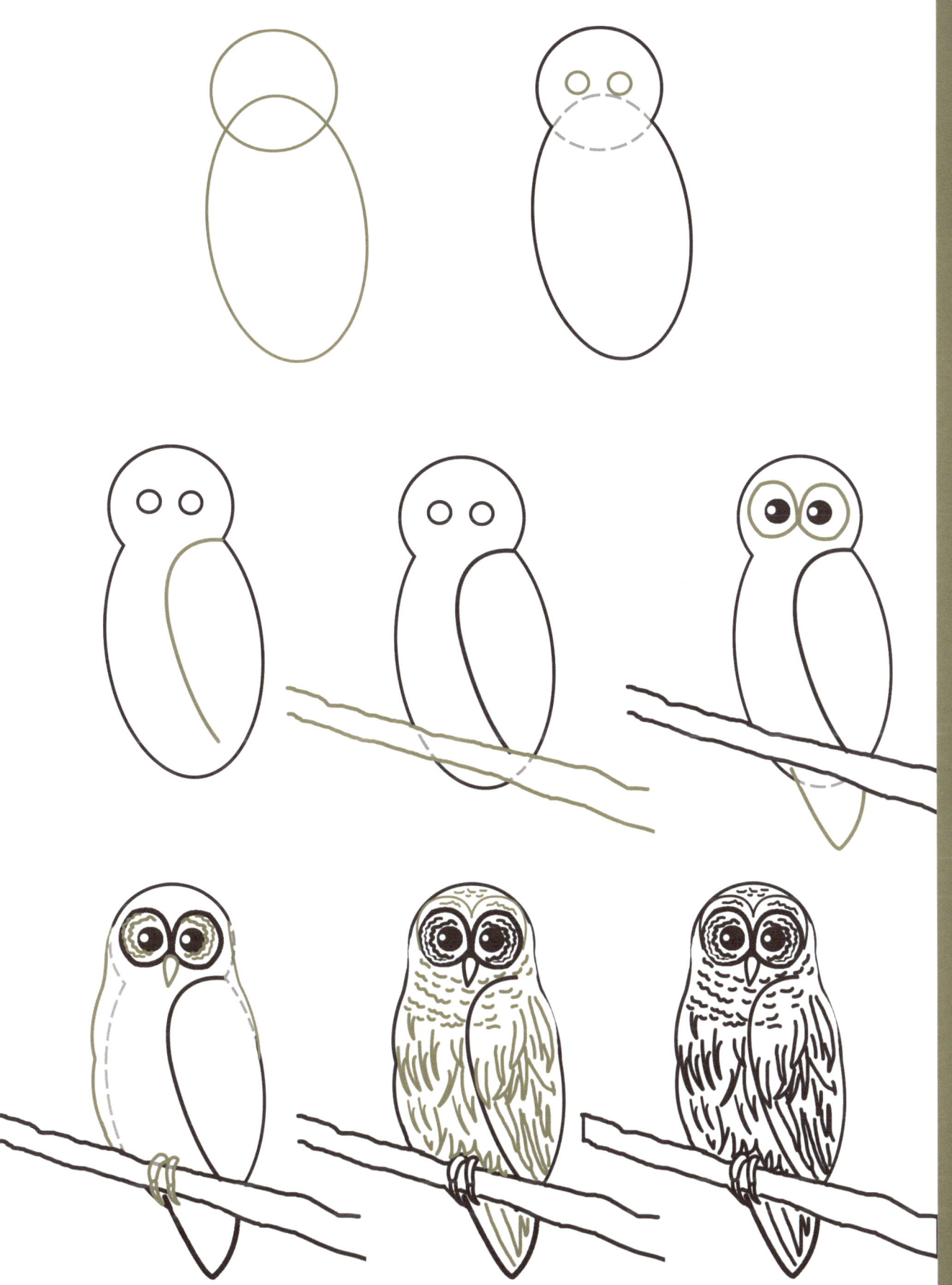

I Heard You Can Draw a...
Ladybug!

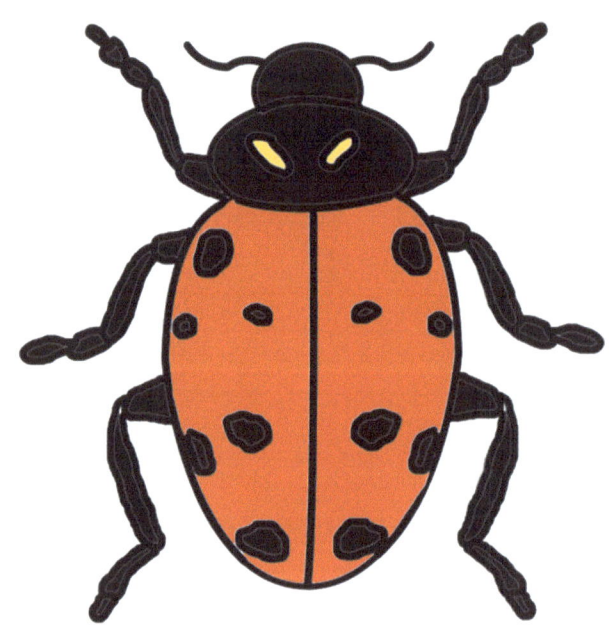

Ladybugs are beetles with six legs. Ladybugs lay eggs underneath leaves. When the eggs hatch, larvae emerge. When the larva is ready, it attaches itself to a leaf and begins the pupa stage. Last, the ladybug emerges!

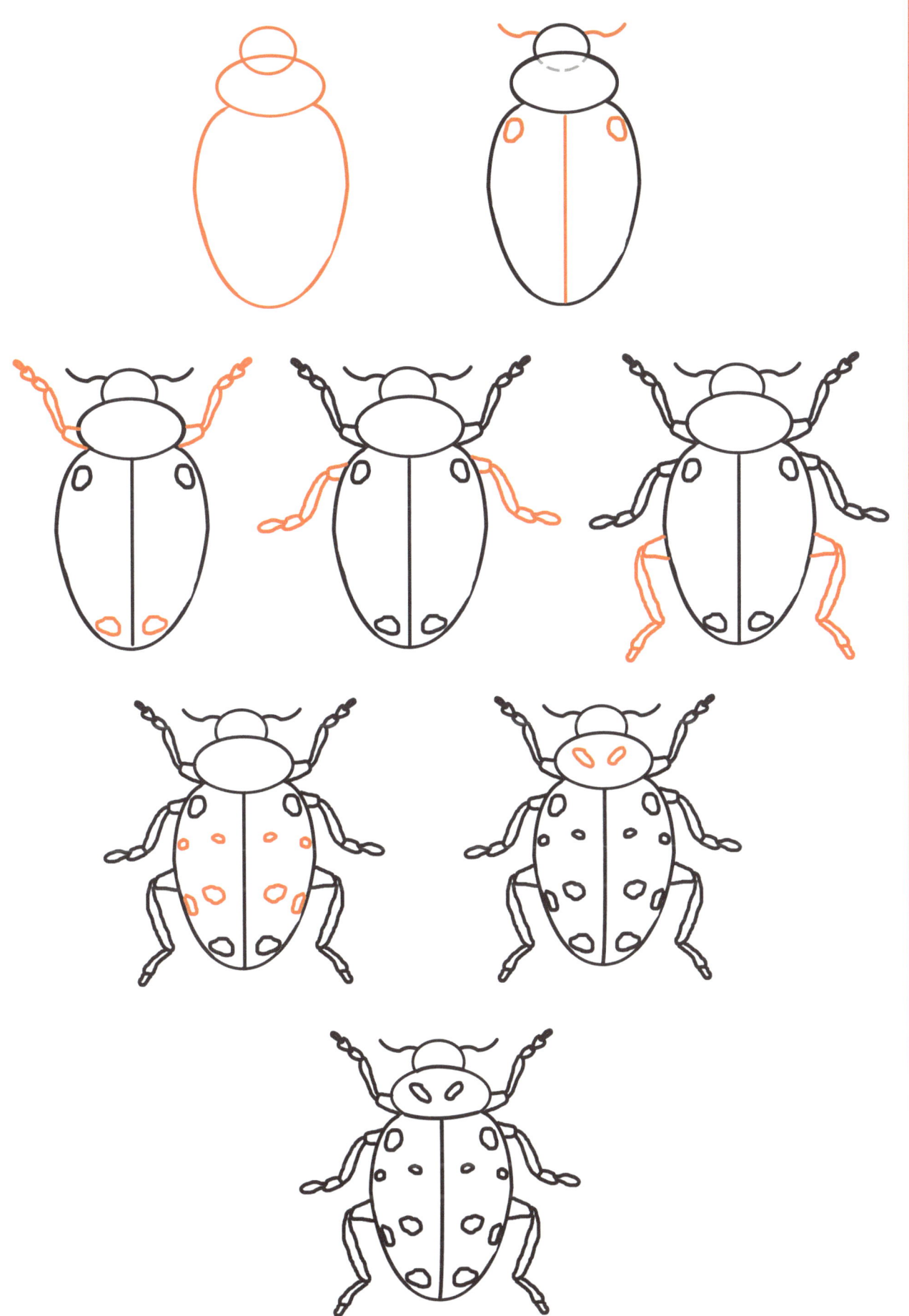

39

I Heard You Can Draw a...
Giant Anteater!

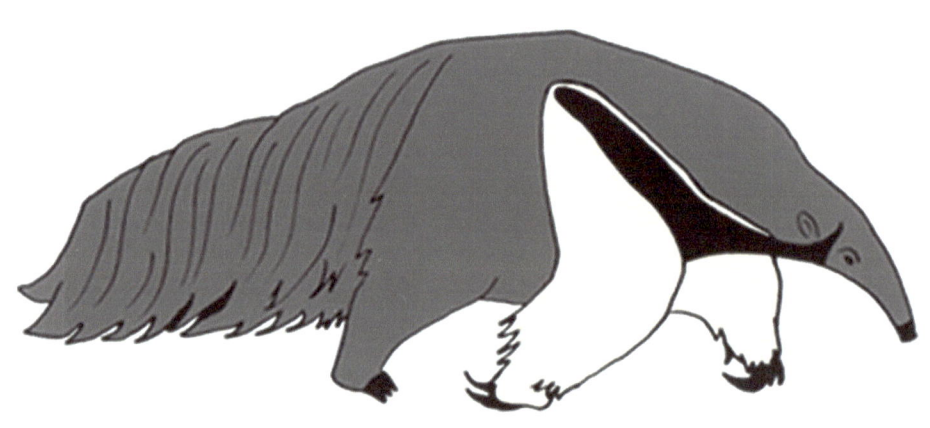

Giant Anteaters live in Central and South America.
They eat thousands of ants each day - up to **30,000** in fact!
They have long tongues that help them eat ants and termites.
Did you notice that they walk on their knuckles?

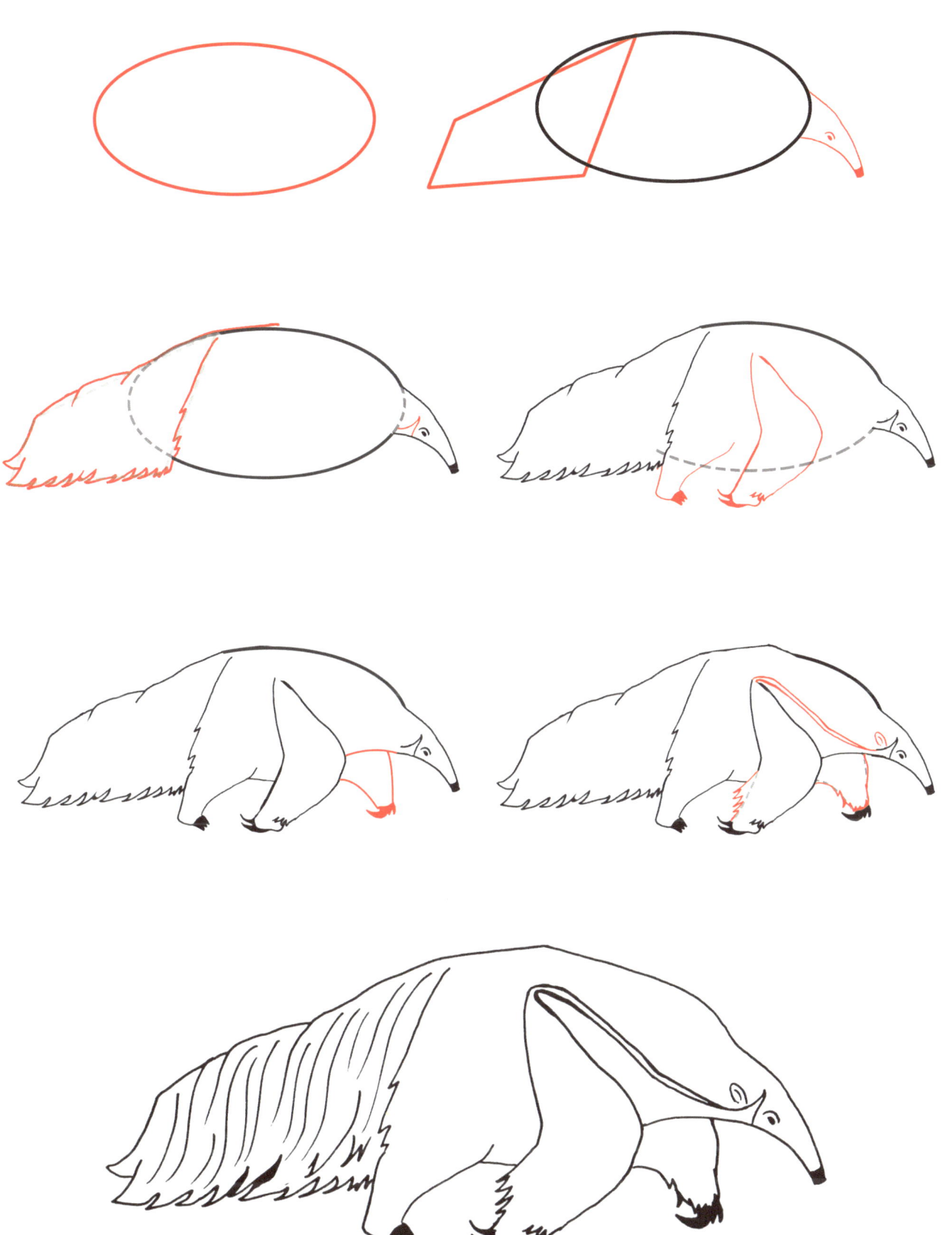

Collect them all!

Visit: IHeardYouCanDraw.tumblr.com

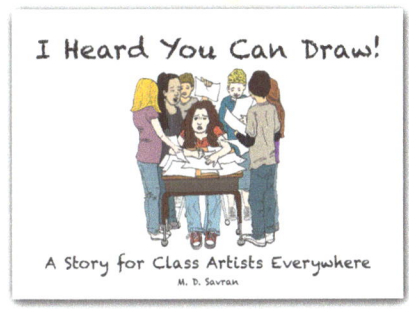

I Heard You Can Draw!
A Story for Class Artists Everywhere
40p Paperback, 10.99

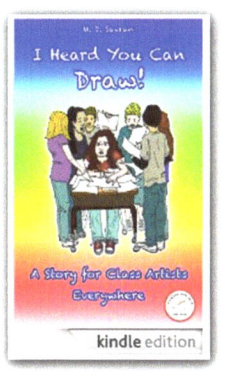

I Heard You Can Draw!
A Story for Class Artists Everywhere
Kindle Edition, 3.99

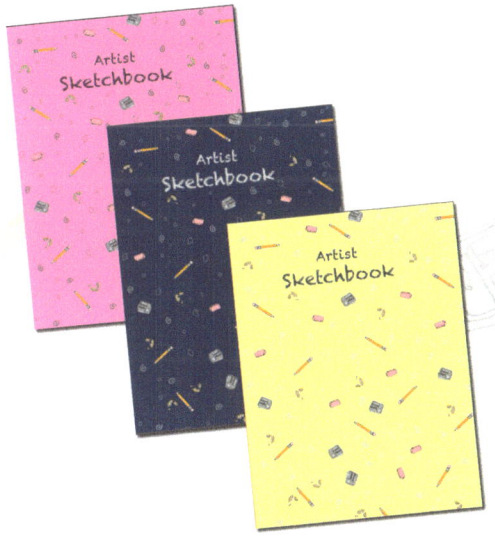

Artist Sketchbook
(Large / Pink / Navy / Yellow)
60 blank pages, 6.99 each

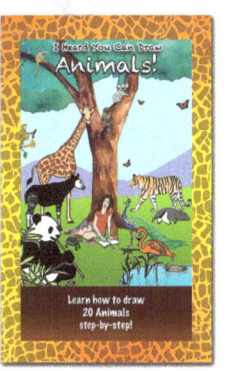

I Heard You Can Draw Animals!
A Step-by-Step Guide
Kindle Edition, 2.99

Index

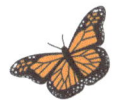

www.ingramcontent.com/pod-product-compliance
Lightning Source LLC
Chambersburg PA
CBHW040748200526
45159CB00023B/1797